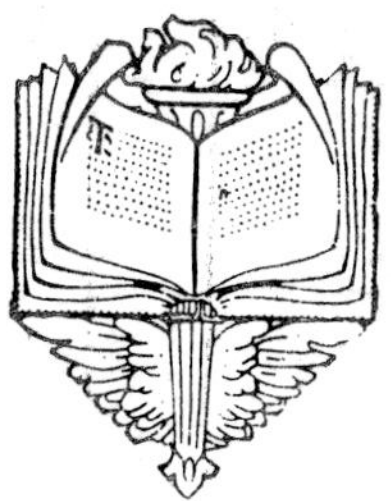

This Volume is placed on our Shelves in honor and memory of

Norma J. Duda

By

Employees of Teledyne Penn Union

Gambridge Springs Public Library Association

GREAT MYSTERIES

Bigfoot

OPPOSING VIEWPOINTS®

Look for these and other exciting *Great Mysteries: Opposing Viewpoints* books:

Animal Communication *by Jacci Cole*
Atlantis *by Wendy Stein*
The Bermuda Triangle *by Norma Gaffron*
Bigfoot *by Norma Gaffron*
Dinosaurs *by Peter and Connie Roop*
ESP *by Michael Arvey*
Pearl Harbor *by Deborah Bachrach*
Poltergeists *by Peter and Connie Roop*
Pyramids *by Barbara Mitchell*
The Shroud of Turin *by Daniel C. Scavone*
The Solar System *by Peter and Connie Roop*
Witches *by Bryna Stevens*

GREAT MYSTERIES

Bigfoot

OPPOSING VIEWPOINTS®

by Norma Gaffron

Greenhaven Press, Inc. San Diego, California

Library of Congress Cataloging-in-Publication Data

Gaffron, Norma, 1931-
Bigfoot : opposing viewpoints.
Bibliography: p.
Includes index.
Summary: Evaluates physical and eyewitness evidence concerning the existence of large, hairy creatures such as the Bigfoot of the Pacific Northwest and the Abominable Snowman of the Himalayas.
1. Yeti-Juvenile literature. [1. Sasquatch. 2. Yeti] I. Title. II. Series: Great mysteries (St. Paul, Minn.)
QL89.2.Y4G34 1989 001.9'44 88-24376
ISBN 0-89908-058-8

San Diego, CA 92128-9009

Dedicated to my son Mike, and the Boy Scouts of Troop 167, from whom I first heard of "The Yeti."

Contents

"When men and women lose the sense of mystery, life will prove to be a gray and dreary business, only with difficulty to be endured."

Harold T. Wilkins, author of Strange Mysteries of Time and Space

Introduction

This book is written for the curious—those who want to explore the mysteries that are everywhere. To be human is to be constantly surrounded by wonderment. How do birds fly? Are ghosts real? Can animals and people communicate? Was King Arthur a real person or a myth? Why did Amelia Earhart disappear? Did history really happen the way we think it did? Where did the world come from? Where is it going?

Great Mysteries: Opposing Viewpoints books are intended to offer the reader an opportunity to explore some of the many mysteries that both trouble and intrigue us. For the span of each book, we want the reader to feel that he or she is a scientist investigating the extinction of the dinosaurs, an archaeologist searching for clues to the origin of the great Egyptian pyramids, a psychic detective testing the existence of ESP.

One thing all mysteries have in common is that there is no ready answer. Often there are *many* answers but none on which even the majority of authorities agrees. *Great Mysteries: Opposing Viewpoints* books introduce the intriguing views of the experts, allowing the reader to participate in their explorations, their theories, and their disagreements as they try to explain the mysteries of our world.

But most readers won't want to stop here. These *Great Mysteries: Opposing Viewpoints* aim to stimulate the reader's curiosity. Although truth is often impossible to discover, the search is fascinating. It is up to the reader to examine the evidence, to decide whether the answer is there—or to explore further.

"Penetrating so many secrets, we cease to believe in the unknowable. But there it sits nevertheless, calmly licking its chops."

H.L. Mencken, American essayist

One

A Mysterious Creature

On a September day in 1941, Mrs. Jeannie Chapman was at home in her cabin in British Columbia, Canada. Her two children, Jimmie and Rosie, were with her. Nothing indicated that this afternoon would be any different from other afternoons. Nothing, that is, until young Jimmie went outdoors to play. Within minutes he rushed back into the house.

"Mummy," he cried. "There's a big cow coming out of the woods!"

Jeannie Chapman heard the fear in her son's voice and looked out the window. What she saw was no cow. Walking on two feet was a hairy creature at least eight feet tall by her estimation. She couldn't tell if it was human or animal.

Mrs. Chapman watched in terror as the creature approached the house. She was momentarily relieved when it went inside a shed on the Chapman property. Without hesitating, she snatched up her children and fled toward the railway station at Ruby Creek. Halfway there she met her husband and the men he was working with laying tracks for the Canadian Pacific Railway. She was so frightened she could hardly describe what she had seen.

A photo of a genuine Bigfoot? Photographer Roger Patterson claims that it is. This is one frame from a piece of movie film shot when Patterson and some friends came upon a Bigfoot in California.

Above: The Chapman cabin in the foothills in British Columbia. After seeing Bigfoot, the family never returned to their home.
Below: The railworkers were also experienced hunters. None of them had ever seen a Bigfoot before.

The men in the railway crew hunted often and were experienced woodsmen. Grabbing their rifles, they headed for the Chapman cabin. They were sure that what Jimmie and his mother had seen was a bear.

The footprints they found told them otherwise. Sixteen inches long and eight inches wide, the prints clearly showed five toes on each foot, like a human's rather than a bear's. And the prints had no claw marks. In the potato patch the impressions were two inches deep in the soil, much deeper than those made by an ordinary person. The men concluded that the monster must have weighed at least three hundred pounds.

The men found a fifty-five-gallon barrel of salted salmon overturned on the Chapman's property. Apparently the creature had found the salmon in the shed, tasted it, but didn't like it. Then it had *lifted* the heavy barrel, carried it outside, and tossed it into the yard. From the yard the creature's tracks led down to the river. Perhaps it had wanted to wash the salt taste out of its mouth before going on.

The tracks went for half a mile, right up to a four-foot-high fence and beyond. Whatever had made the tracks had taken this obstacle without breaking stride

Measuring Bigfoot's stride. This picture was taken in the state of Washington, an area with many reported Bigfoot sightings.

as there was no indication that it had climbed the fence. On the other side of the fence, the tracks went on until they were no longer visible on the rocky ground at the bottom of Ruby Bluffs.

The men, by now as upset as Jeannie Chapman, consulted other experienced woodsmen. George Cousins, a telegraph operator at Ruby Creek, studied the tracks. He said they were three times bigger than any bear tracks he had ever seen. Joe Dunn, deputy sheriff of neighboring Whatcom County, also inspected and measured the tracks. He reported, "I am well satisfied that these tracks are not those of a bear." He thought they resembled those that a flat-footed human with fallen arches would make.

The Chapman family had heard—and seen—enough. They never returned to their cabin.

What was the "monster" that frightened Jimmie Chapman and his mother? Was it an unknown animal that lived hidden in the forest? Or was it a wild human

"I deny the existence of Bigfoot."

Vadim Ranov, explorer

"I don't see how it could be a hoax."

Wayne King, founder of the Michigan-Canadian Bigfoot Center

who had wandered out of the woods?

This was not the first report of huge, hairy, humanlike creatures in the Pacific Northwest. For hundreds of years, Indians in Canada have told stories of a ferocious-looking wild creature of the woods. They call it *Sasquatch*, or "hairy giant." In California and the northwestern United States, this creature is called *Bigfoot*. Similar creatures, found under a variety of names, are described in the folklore of many North, Central, and South American Indians.

Indians, however, are not the only people who have seen these giants of the forest. Travelers, workers, and others who have never heard Indian tales have reported encounters with huge, mysterious animals. Descriptions vary, but the following is typical: Sasquatch or Bigfoot is said to be a hairy, brown, humanlike creature eight feet tall or more, weighing up to one thousand pounds. It walks upright and takes six- to eight-foot strides. It leaves footprints up to twenty-four inches long and eight inches wide. The footprints are almost identical in shape to those of a human, but they are several inches deep on surfaces where a heavy man makes scarcely a mark.

Two other characteristics often mentioned are a high-pitched whistling scream sometimes heard when a Bigfoot is nearby, and a terrible odor. In short, Bigfoot stinks!

Does Bigfoot Really Exist?

Although thousands of footprints have been found, a Bigfoot has never been captured. Sightings of the creature and its tracks are not enough to prove its existence. Plaster casts have been made of many of the footprints; scientists say these are interesting, but footprints can be faked. Examination of bits of hair found on bushes and trees has proved nothing either.

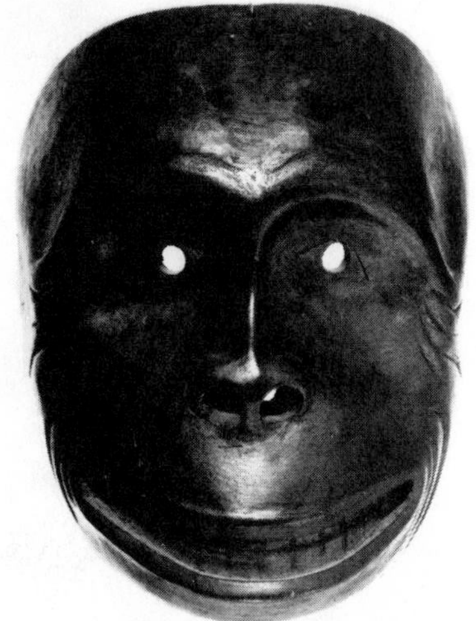

An Indian mask from the Northwest United States. Some say Sasquatch looks like this.

Although Bigfoot has been reported in many areas of North America, this coastal region is where the majority of the sightings have been.

Droppings have been found and attributed to Bigfoot. But analysis of the excrement has not revealed what sort of creature left it, only what that creature had eaten.

People who claim to have seen Bigfoot or Sasquatch swear they are telling the truth. In some cases, such as the Chapmans', at least two people saw the giant at the same time. Their stories are identical. Don Hunter, author of the book, *Sasquatch*, says the Chapman sighting is significant because "It was, according to records, the first voluntary visit by the creature to what we call civilization, and the first time that a substantial set of tracks was viewed by a number of persons from various walks of life, including a police official." But the question remains: *What* did they see?

René Dahinden, a Canadian adventurer, has devoted over twenty years to establishing whether Sasquatch exists or not. He believes a creature of enormous size could survive in the Pacific Northwest. It could get food from the forests, the mountain streams, and the ocean beaches. Because thousands of square miles of this area have never been explored, a Sasquatch could easily stay hidden. Dahinden has not come to any

Opposite page: Hunter Phil Thompson measures a Bigfoot footprint he found in Oregon. It measured 17 inches long and 7 inches wide. Below: Bigfoot seeker John Green with plaster casts of Bigfoot footprints. Scientists wonder how many Bigfoot prints are genuine and how many are fake.

Left: The dense woods of the Pacific Northwest are said to be the home of Bigfoot. Below: A road sign in the state of Washington.

conclusions, but his hopes for finding a Sasquatch are high.

Scientist and author Ivan T. Sanderson believes that primitive, humanlike creatures definitely exist in the modern world. He lists at least three types. The first, which he calls *Neanderthaler*, or caveman type, is found in Mongolia, China, and Tibet. The second, the large creature known as Bigfoot or Sasquatch, is found in North America, Central America, and possibly South America. The third type, the beastlike *Meh-Teh*, is the size of an average human, but has twelve-inch fangs. The Meh-Teh is the "Abominable Snowman" said to roam the Himalaya Mountains in Asia. Sanderson is convinced that this abominable snowman is a beast remaining from "a most ancient side-branch of both our own and the apes' family tree and more likely from the twig of the apes than from our lot.''

Other scientists want more solid evidence before they will spend time or money searching for the creature. Scientist Grover S. Krantz says that ''only an actual specimen'' will satisfy him. Even a dead one would do.

But Dr. John Napier, author and former director of primate biology at the Smithsonian Institution, says, ''I am convinced the Sasquatch exists.''

Who is right?

Are the people who have seen a Sasquatch lying? Or are they just ''seeing things''? Is it all a joke? Is someone playing a trick, dressing up as a hairy beast to scare people in the woods?

What—or who—is making those footprints?

What—or who—lurks just out of sight in the wilderness areas of the world?

''Not even a single bone has been identified as belonging to this species.''

Grover S. Krantz, scientist

''Hunters in Africa have written that they have never heard of anybody coming upon a dead elephant, either.''

Alan Landsburg, author

Two

A Tradition of Terror

The area in North America that is said to be Bigfoot's habitat, or home, covers more than 125,000 square miles of dense forest. It includes the states of Oregon and Washington, part of northern California, part of northern Idaho, and extends into much of British Columbia in Canada.

This is rugged country. High mountain peaks are permanently covered with snow. Ice-cold streams snake through deep valleys and gorges. In his book, *The Search for Bigfoot*, Peter Byrne writes that there are deep ravines "that never hear the voice of Man." It is not surprising that people long ago wondered what secrets, and what secret creatures, were hidden in this great wilderness.

Indian Legends

According to anthropologist Thomas Buckley, Bigfoot seems to have been "a figure of some concern in native northwestern California since aboriginal times." The Karok Indians, for example, told about "upslope persons" which were apparently the Indian version of Bigfoot. These upslope persons were "hairy, large, strong, stupid, and crude," and lived

Bigfoot country in the Northwestern United States and Canada is rugged country.

Bigfoot seeker Réne Dahinden stands beside a lifesize statue of Bigfoot at Willow Creek, California. Dahinden is 5'10''; Bigfoot is 8' tall.

in rocky dells far up in the mountains.

Upslope persons could be dangerous so Indians had to be wary. In one folktale, the children of Long-Billed Dowitcher (a dowitcher is a wading bird like a sandpiper) were captured and eaten by an upslope person. Long-Billed Dowitcher in turn killed the upslope and restored his children to life by "soaking their bones in a power-granting alpine lake near the monster's lair."

But not all giants in Indian folktales were bad. In a Yurok Indian story a young woman disappeared from a village near present-day Bluff Creek, California. When she reappeared, she carried a newborn child. She also had with her five baskets of dentalia shells, or tooth shells—valuable items in the Yurok culture. She had married a giant, "one of four brothers who stepped from ridge to ridge and shouted loudly." When Yurok Indians tell this story today, they say she married Bigfoot.

Perhaps the hairy giant in the Indian legends is the Bigfoot of today. Maybe those legends are not myths, but true stories of real happenings. Whatever the creatures are, some people think one of them might have caused a tragedy recounted by Theodore Roosevelt in his book *Wilderness Hunter.* Roosevelt told what happened to a man named Baumann in the mid-1800s. According to Roosevelt, Baumann "could hardly repress a shudder" as he recounted his experience.

Fear in the Forest

Baumann and a fellow trapper were camping in the woods. They saw animal tracks near their campsite, but paid no attention to them, thinking they had been made by a bear. When they returned from trapping and found their shelter torn apart, they thought a bear had done that, too. But while Baumann was making supper, his companion examined the footprints more closely.

"The most distressing tendency I find . . . is the continual reference to the day when a specimen is brought in."

Gordon S. Strasenburg, scientist

"Some people say they only want (to document the existence of) Bigfoot and not capture it, but how can they say they have no interest in taking one?"

Wayne King, founder of the Michigan-Canadian Bigfoot Center

Teddy Roosevelt, who was President of the United States from 1901 to 1909, was an avid explorer and adventurer. He reported a convincing story of a mysterious and destructive creature. Was it a Bigfoot?

"Baumann, that bear has been walking on two legs," he said. Baumann laughed, but his partner insisted he was right. They discussed the possibility of the footprints having been made by a human being and concluded that they had not been. The two men then repaired their lean-to, rolled up in their blankets, and went to sleep.

Then, wrote Roosevelt, "At midnight Baumann was awakened by some noise and sat up in his blankets. As he did so his nostrils were struck by a strong wild-beast odour and he caught the loom of a great body in the darkness at the mouth of the lean-to. Grasping his rifle he fired at the vague, threatening shadow, but must have missed, for immediately afterwards he heard the smashing of the underwood as the thing, whatever it was, rushed off into the impenetrable blackness of the forest and night."

The men built up their fire and huddled beside it until dawn. But in the bright morning sunlight, being afraid seemed silly. So they agreed to gather their traps before they left the area. It would have been better for them if they had just packed their camping gear

Above: A muskrat trapper at work. Right: As Baumann made supper at the campfire, his friend examined the mysterious tracks more closely. Was the mysterious visitor a bear—or a Bigfoot?

and left.

Toward late afternoon Baumann offered to gather the last three beaver traps while his companion went on to the campsite to pack their things.

The sun was low in the sky when Baumann returned. He could see that a campfire had been built and had gone out, leaving thin blue smoke still curling upward. Baumann shouted. No answer. Then,

> his eye fell on the body of his friend, stretched beside the trunk of a great fallen spruce. Rushing towards it the horrified trapper found that the body was still warm, but that the neck was broken, while there were four great fang marks in the throat.
>
> The footprints of the unknown beast, printed deep in the soft soil, told the whole story. . . . It had not eaten the body, but apparently had romped and gambolled around it in uncouth and ferocious glee, occasionally rolling it over and over; and had then fled back into the soundless depths of the woods.

> Baumann, utterly unnerved . . . abandoned everything but his rifle and struck off at top speed down the pass, not halting until he reached the beaver meadows where the hobbled ponies were still grazing. Mounting, he rode onwards through the night, until far beyond the reach of pursuit.

Roosevelt does not say what he thought the creature was that killed Baumann's partner. He only tells the story. But other people have asked: Could it have been a Bigfoot that ended the man's life, or was it just a bear? And why did it kill Baumann's partner?

Captured by a Bigfoot

In the decades that followed, more frightening tales were told. In 1924, something happened to a lumberjack named Albert Ostman that he never forgot. That year, Ostman decided to take a vacation and go prospecting for gold.

According to Peter Byrne in his book, *The Search for Bigfoot,* Ostman had never heard of Bigfoot before an Indian guide on his trip told him that "the

A Yukon gold prospector. Lumberjack Albert Ostman got more than he bargained for when he went gold prospecting.

Sasquatch are big people living in the mountains.'' The guide refused to stay with Ostman; he insisted on going back home before nightfall.

While Ostman was asleep on his third night out, he says something picked him up and carried him off. The thing must have been very strong, for it carried Ostman, his rifle, and his knapsack, all still in his sleeping bag. It carried its burden for ''what seemed to be three hours,'' uphill and down. When Ostman was finally dropped to the ground, he saw he was in a small grassy clearing surrounded by mountains.

Then, according to Byrne, Ostman ''was confronted with four large Bigfeet, who stood around him chattering to each other.'' It was still dark and Ostman could not see them clearly. At dawn, they ''looked like humans to him, rather than apes.'' They appeared to be a family: a father, mother, and two children. Ostman described the large male as about eight feet tall with huge arms and legs. He had very long forearms and large hands. His fingernails were short and broad. All members of the family were covered with hair except for their feet, the palms of their hands, their noses, and their eyelids. Their feet were padded underneath like a dog's. Ostman estimated the weight of the large male to be over 700 pounds, and the female close to 550 pounds. Ostman says he stayed with the family for almost a week. He ate food from his pack and slept in his sleeping bag. The family of giants slept on a cave floor with what ''seemed to be blankets, woven of cedar bark and packed with dry moss.'' They did not harm Ostman, but watched him constantly. He felt uneasy.

Ostman waited for a chance to escape. It finally came when he got the family interested in the snuff he carried. They ate the powdered tobacco, which was meant for sniffing, then screamed in pain. Taking his rifle, Ostman ''made for the opening in the canyon wall. The female attempted to come after him, but he fired a shot over her head and she ran back to the

''My last thought is that we probably need the sasquatch as much as he needs us. He is, after all, a most human animal.''

Richard Beeson, scientist

''If it is his brain that distinguishes Homo sapiens from his animal relatives, then the sasquatch is an animal—an upright ape—and nothing more.''

John Green, reporter

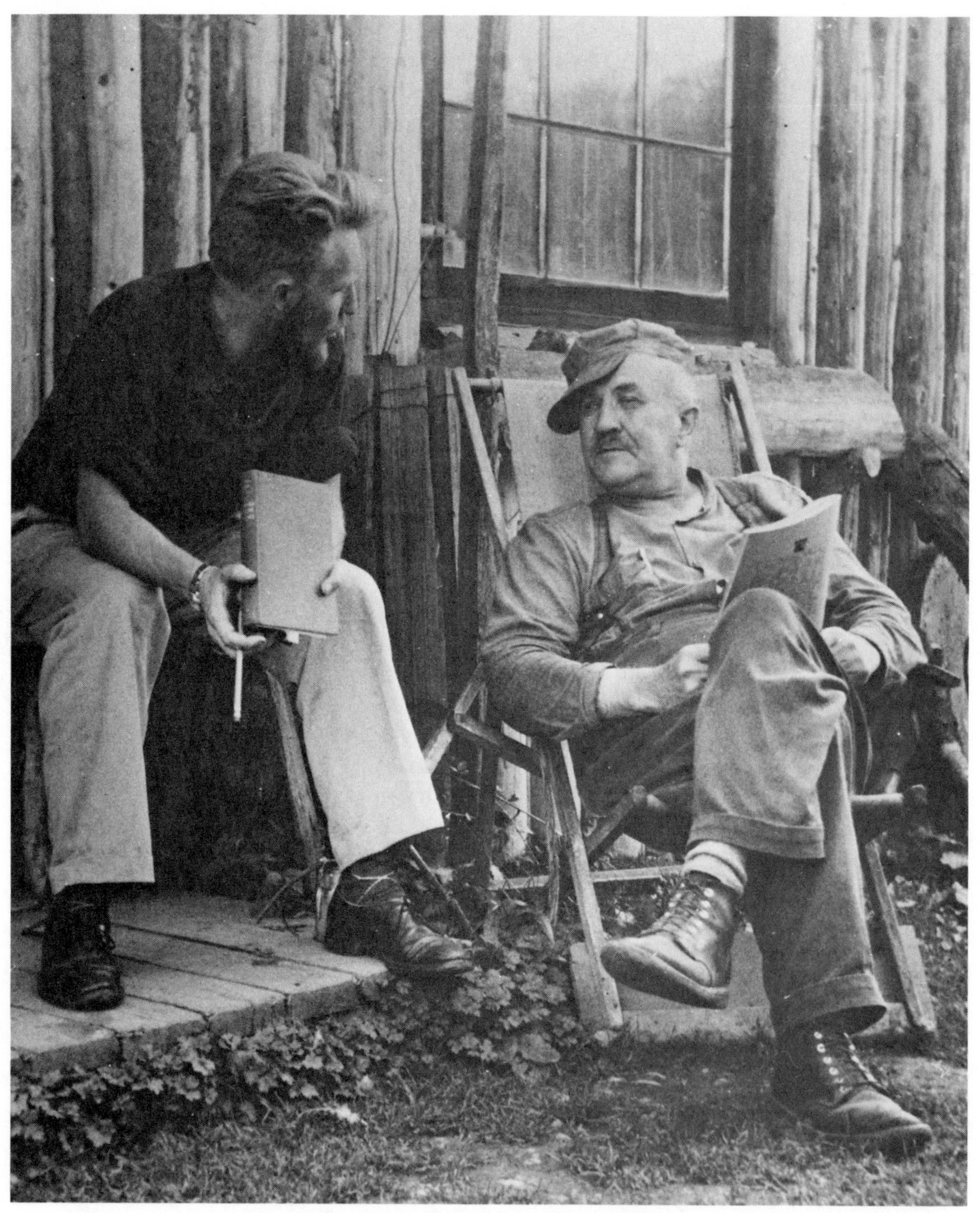

Opposite page: Explorer René Dahinden chats with Albert Ostman who claimed he was kidnapped by a Bigfoot family. Left: "Smokeless tobacco," or snuff. The Bigfoot family's fascination with this allowed Ostman to get away.

lair."

After his escape, Ostman kept his story secret for many years. He thought no one would believe him. Then in 1957 a rash of newspaper stories of Bigfoot sightings were printed. Ostman decided he too would tell of his experience. People listened and wondered. Was Ostman's story true?

According to Byrne, "There was a great deal more detail in Ostman's original account of his experience, and to my way of thinking, the more detail there is, the more believable a story is."

When Ostman told his story to Justice of the Peace Lieutenant Colonel A.M. Naismith, Naismith said he "found Albert Ostman to be in full possession of his mental faculties, of pleasant manner, and with a good sense of humor." Naismith added, "Ostman certainly believed the story himself."

Primate biologist Dr. John Napier finds one aspect of the story that "does not ring true." Ostman said the Sasquatch family ate "grasses with sweet roots, spruce and hemlock tips and tubers that the mother and son collected." He saw no evidence of meat eating. Napier suggests that creatures of this size would need a more substantial diet.

In *The Mysterious World: An Atlas of the Unexplained*, Francis Hitching disagrees. He says, "Odd though it may seem, the coniferous mountain forests of the North American continent are largely unexplored, and there is no compelling reason why a quite large population of unknown beasts should not exist there, surviving on a frugal and mostly vegetarian diet."

What do the Sasquatch live on? Do they need meat? Is that why they kidnapped Ostman—for the main course of their Saturday night barbecue?

Dr. John Napier doubts that these giants could survive without meat, but of stories such as Ostman's

Dr. John Napier studies primates—humans, apes, gorillas, and chimps—and Bigfoot. Here he holds a plaster cast of a Bigfoot footprint in California.

he says, ''Eyewitness reports which provide strictly circumstantial evidence are very persuasive.'' He offers no opinons on the Bigfoot's motives in the Ostman case but adds, "There must be something in north-west America that needs explaining, and that something leaves man-like footprints.''

Construction worker Jerry Crew would agree.

No Joke

Albert Ostman may have told his story as a joke. He may have been playing a trick. But if someone was playing a trick on Gerald ''Jerry'' Crew in 1958, he didn't laugh. Nor did the foreman of Jerry's road construction job in northwestern California.

Jerry operated the bulldozer that did the first-stage clearing for roadways through the forest. He and the rest of the crew were working on a road that was in such rugged country it had been surveyed only from the air.

A 15½ inch human-like footprint photographed by explorer Peter Byrne.

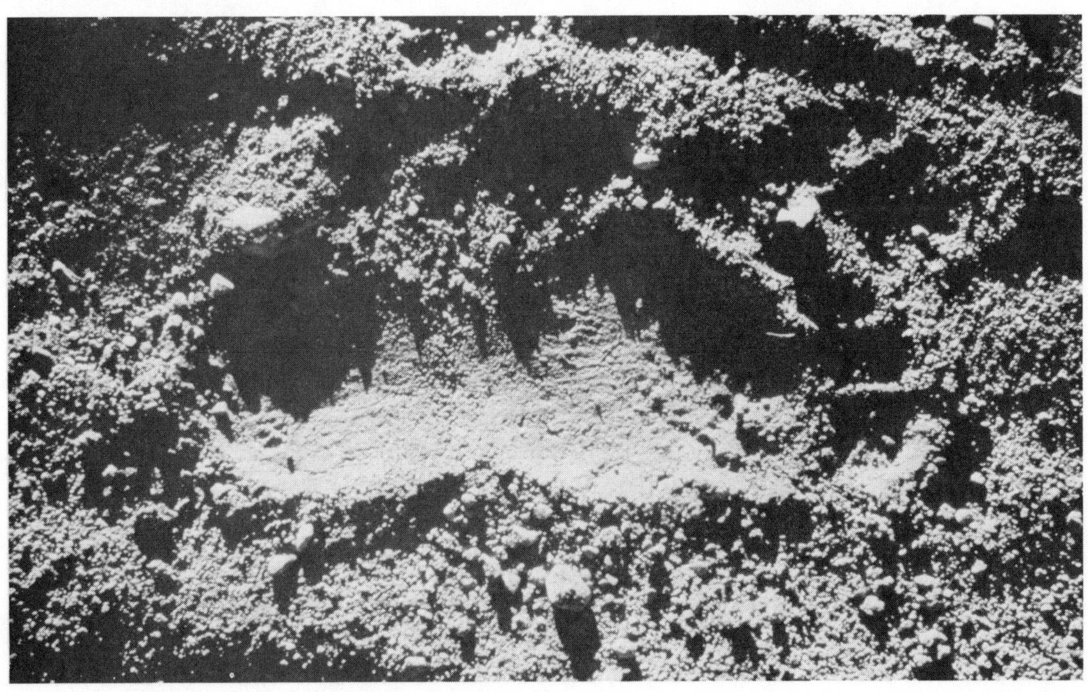

Bulldozer operator Jerry Crew and his co-workers found signs of a Bigfoot near their worksite.

During the week, the road-building crew lived at campsites near the head of the road. Most of the men returned to their homes in nearby towns each weekend. A few of the workers brought in trailers so their families could vacation in the woods. Their campsite was ten miles behind the head of the road. Jerry Crew drove home on weekends to be with his family in the small town of Willow Creek.

On Friday, August 24, Crew was the last to leave for home because he worked about one-quarter of a mile beyond the others. He ran the bulldozer back and forth over newly scraped earth before driving it down the mountain to his pickup truck. The only tracks he left in the soft, damp earth were those of the tractor and his own boots.

Mysterious Footprints

On Monday morning, August 27, Crew returned to work. At the campsite he saw the job foreman standing in the doorway of the shack that served as an office. Crew tapped his horn lightly in greeting, and the foreman waved casually. Crew went on up the mountain and parked near the bulldozer. He was a little early so he stood for a moment in the stillness of the forest. The air was fragrant with the scent of pine and cedar trees. Peaceful. Crew breathed deeply of the fresh air, then put on his hard hat.

As he strolled toward his machine, Crew noticed a large footprint in the dirt. He saw a second and a third. Bear tracks, he thought. But then from the high seat of his bulldozer, Crew looked down and saw a whole line of footprints approaching the bulldozer. They circled the machine, then continued down the outer edge of the raw roadway. One long look told him these tracks were larger than any he had ever seen, and they were unmistakably shaped like a human foot.

Crew quickly checked to see if the bulldozer had been tampered with. He switched on the engine. Nothing wrong there. He turned it off and jumped to the ground. He stared disbelievingly at the footprints, dry and crusted in the soil that had been damp on Friday.

When he noticed how small his own tracks looked beside the large ones, Crew broke out in goose pimples. These were the footprints of a giant. He tried to walk in the tracks, but they were too far apart. He had to jump from print to print to stay in the tracks.

All his life Crew had heard tales of crazy hermits who lived alone in the woods and of wild people loose

Four typical footprints compared. Left to right: gorilla, Bigfoot, human, bear.

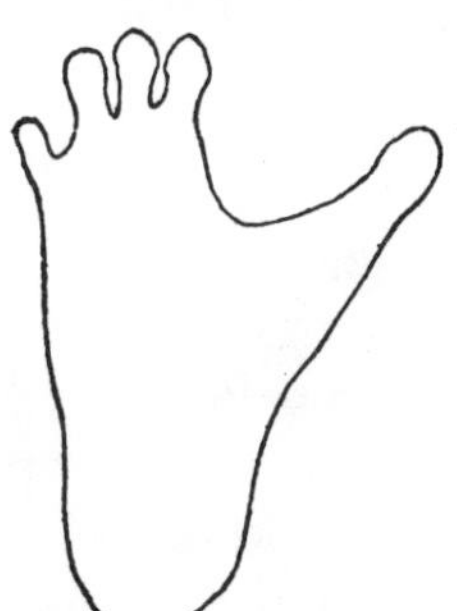

Bigfoot eyewitnesses from the Pacific Northwest. Left to right: Sgt. Larry Gamache, Kathy Gamache, Bob Gimlin, Grover and Millie Kiggins. Each of these people claim to have seen Bigfoot at least once.

in the forest. He had never taken these stories seriously. And he wasn't going to take these tracks seriously either. Some of his friends must have come up here, made the huge tracks, and then left. But he wondered which man, tired after working all week on the road, would bother to come up here for a joke. And what stranger would come this far up an unfinished road to play a trick on someone he or she didn't even know?

Only two sets of tracks were visible, the big-footed ones and his own. Crew was so uneasy that he hurried back to his truck and reported to this foreman, Wilbur Wallace.

Other Incidents

Wallace listened. He recalled an incident that had occurred on a construction job the previous summer: A mechanic had reported that a fifty-five-gallon metal drum filled with diesel oil was missing. Only the deep round depression made by the 450-pound container remained in the soft dirt at the edge of the road. Huge

footprints were found that time, too. The mechanic had followed the prints into the woods to a spot where the heavy drum had apparently been set down. If someone had rolled the drum, no disturbed ground or broken shrubs showed it. The owner of the huge footprints must have carried the container, because the mechanic saw the bright orange drum over the edge of a drop-off. No snapped twigs or broken shrubs indicated that it had been rolled down the hill. To have landed where it did, it must have been *tossed* far out over the edge of the cliff.

That time Wallace and the mechanic had agreed not to mention the mysterious happening to the other workers. If the workers imagined some monster roaming the woods, they might become frightened and quit the job.

With the additional evidence of the footprints Crew had found, Wallace could no longer put the problem from his mind. Besides, he now remembered that a

700-pound spare tire for the grading machine had been found at the bottom of a deep ravine two weeks earlier. He and the workers had assumed some vandals had pushed it off the road.

Still, Wallace tried to shrug off this new incident. None of the families camping in the woods had reported any strange noises over the weekend. No one had seen anything unusual. When the other workers learned of the footprints, one of them laughed and said it was probably an ape escaped from a circus. Wallace laughed too. He told them to get back to work and to let him know if they came upon any apes in the timber.

Things were quiet until a newspaper in Eureka, California, published Crew's story. Dozens of other stories followed. Everyone seemed to have seen mysterious footprints at one time or another.

Then, on October 1, Jerry Crew saw tracks again. When he reported them to Wallace, two workmen quit

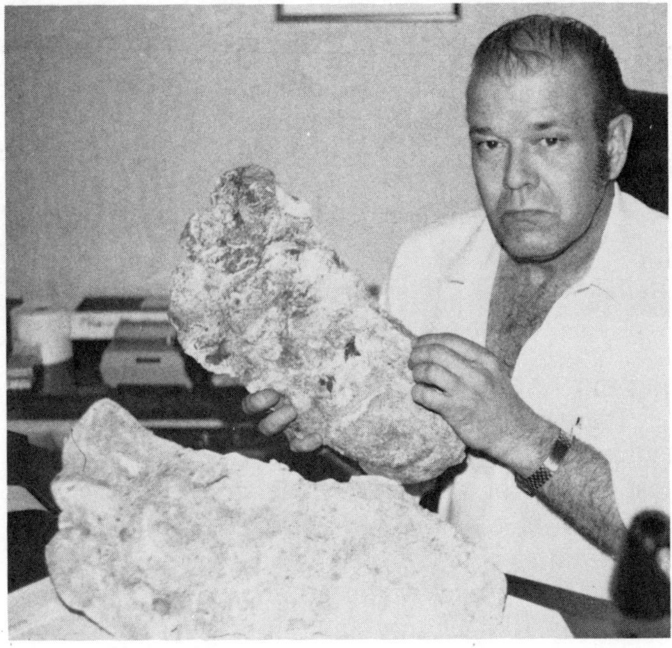

Bigfoot has been seen in many parts of North America. Opposite page: Bob Jones, president of a group that explores unusual natural phenomena, holds a cast of a Bigfoot print found in Louisiana in the southern part of the United States. Left: Wayne King of the Michigan/Canadian Bigfoot Center holds a cast of a Bigfoot print found in Michigan in the North Central United States.

Wayne King compared a human foot to a Bigfoot print. Could a human-like creature exist with such big feet?

and moved their families out of the mountains.

But some people were still laughing. They refused to take the footprints seriously. Crew made a plaster cast of one of the giant-sized barefoot tracks. He showed it to the workers still on the job. They decided that since the creature had shown no signs of hurting them, they would go on working.

When Jerry Crew and his plaster cast were

photographed for the front page of *The Humboldt Times* newspaper, the editor characterized Crew as a hardworking, sober, steady man. People divided into two groups over the issue; some thought the tracks were real, others thought it was all a practical joke.

In her book, *On the Track of Bigfoot*, Marian T. Place says, "Consider this: Jerry Crew did not make a plaster cast from something he imagined."

The forested mountains of the Pacific Northwest are not the only place where huge hairy monsters, real or imagined, are a source of terror and mystery.

Does Bigfoot have relatives living in other countries?

Apparently so.

"So great is the popular desire to believe the unbelievable that there is a tendency for the most unlikely stories based upon the slenderest evidence to gain widespread acceptance."

Eric Shipton, mountaineer

"I am ready to accept that people are capable of imagining things—but imagination does not create unclassifiable footprints."

Myra Shackley, author

Three

Bigfoot's Cousins

Halfway around the world from Bigfoot territory, in the Himalayan country of Nepal, natives are careful to avoid encountering a hairy beast known as the *yeti*, or "snowman." The yeti has an abominable smell, just as Bigfoot does. Thus it is called the "Abominable Snowman," a name some authors use interchangeably with "Bigfoot." Both mean any large half-human, half-animal creature found in out-of-the-way places.

The Yeti

Among the natives of Nepal is a tribe of particularly hardy people known as the Sherpa. The Sherpa often serve as guides because they are familiar with the mountain environment. Yet for hundreds of years they have been frightened of a hairy beast that no one can identify. This creature they call the yeti lives up where the air is thin and cold and the snow never melts. It leaves mysterious footprints similar to those of Bigfoot. In many stories it is no more than six feet tall—about the size of a human. In other stories it is as tall as fifteen feet! The American Bigfoot is almost always said to be about eight feet tall. Perhaps the yeti and Bigfoot are relatives.

A yeti, drawn by a Tibetan artist.

This map shows some of the area where Bigfoot creatures are most frequently reported.

According to the Sherpa, three breeds, or types, of yeti exist: the *Teh-Ima,* the *Meh-Teh*, and the *Duz-Teh*.

The Teh-Ima

The Teh-Ima is the smallest of the three. It is about four or five feet tall. Its tracks are about four inches long and are found only in the lower mountain regions. In some books Teh-Ima is spelled *Thelma*. Mountaineer and journalist Desmond Doig says, "The Thelma is most certainly a monkey." He compares it to the Pyar-them monkey of the neighboring regions of Sikkim, Bhutan, and southeast Tibet. The Pyar-them, or "little man," "hoots through the jungles, piling twigs and leaves into neat bundles on the forest floor."

The Teh-Ima is not as frightening to the natives as the bigger yeti.

The Meh-Teh

The Meh-Teh is "the meanest beast in the Himalayas," according to author Barbara Antonopulos. In her book *The Abominable Snowman* she states,

An artist's comparison of the sizes of the American Bigfoot and the three yetis observed by Sherpas.

"When people speak of the Abominable Snowman, the Meh-Teh is probably the type they mean."

The Meh-Teh walks on two legs, like Bigfoot does. It has a pointed head and either large square teeth or long fangs. The beast's hair can be red, brown, gray, black, or white. Dr. John Napier says that according to the stories told, the hair below the knee is often a different color from that of the rest of the body. This characteristic is also mentioned in stories of Bigfoot.

Author Ivan T. Sanderson includes the Meh-Teh in his list of primitive creatures. He reports that the Meh-Teh eats plants, small animals, insects, and young birds. The Sherpa aren't sure what it eats, but they shiver and retreat when they see its tracks. They believe that even if the Meh-Teh doesn't eat people, it may attack those who wander into its territory.

The Duz-Teh

The third and largest yeti, the Duz-Teh, looks much like a bear and is usually described as being six to eight feet tall. It sometimes walks on all fours. The Duz-Teh is mainly a plant-eater, but it has been

"Indications seem stronger than ever that we are dealing with 'Animal X,' an unknown variety, or possibly species, a dangerous beast of marked ferocity, who has little to commend him."

Ralph Izzard, author

"I bet Bigfoot is a mischievous Yogi Bear."

Clive Cussler, author

accused of killing animals. In *Monsters*, author Rhoda Blumberg says this type of yeti "usually eats yaks," which are large oxlike animals. Blumberg warns that any stray human may be in danger too, "for the Duz-Teh may also be a people-eater."

How Dangerous Are the Yeti?

Antonopulos recounts a story of some Norwegian mountain climbers who came upon a creature in the Zemu Pass in eastern Nepal. The men froze in terror. "Heading straight at them was an ugly, ape-like creature. Were they imagining it—or was the creature making an eerie, whistling sound?" Before they could ponder the answer, writes Antonopulos, the beast attacked one of the men, knocking him down and tearing at his flesh. When the other men rushed to help their companion, the beast glared at them and disappeared among the rocks and snow.

A Sherpa tribesman named Tensing Norgay

Mt. Everest, the formidable mountain scaled by Sir Edmund Hillary and his party. Yetis have often been reported on Mt. Everest, in the Himalaya mountain chain.

Tensing Norgay, the Sherpa herdsman and mountain guide, whose father saw a yeti. Norgay traveled on Sir Edmund Hillary's expedition.

claimed that his father once encountered a yeti. The beast had reddish fur, an apelike face, and a pointed head. It had a terrible temper and threw stones at the yaks Norgay's father was herding. Norgay's father drove the beast away by building a fire. The physical description indicates that this was a Meh-Teh, but the attack on the yaks is more characteristic of a Duz-Teh. Norgay said the Sherpa would not be concerned about which type it was. They avoid both. The Sherpa say even the *eyes* of the yeti are dangerous. Their eyes are large and deeply sunken, and glow like red-hot coals. A legend warns that a person who looks into the eyes of a yeti will die.

Though the people of Nepal are afraid of the yeti, they accept it as part of their lives. According to Alan Landsburg, author of *In Search of Myths and Monsters*, the Sherpa say, "We have many wild animals here; there are wolves, bears, yetis, snow leopards, rabbits and many others."

But the other animals don't have eyes with deadly power. Why is the yeti different?

The natives don't wonder why, but visitors to these snowy peaks often do. One of the first stories of the mysterious yeti to reach Europe was an account told by a Greek photographer, N.A. Tombazi.

Opposite page: A yeti footprint found in the Himalayas. Compare its size to the hiking boot of an average-size man.

Tombazi's Story

In 1925, N.A. Tombazi was serving as a member of a British geographical expedition in the Himalayas. He and his companions were at an altitude of 15,000 feet when one of their guides pointed to something odd moving across the lower slopes. Tombazi recalled:

> The intense glare and brightness of the snow prevented me from seeing anything for the first few seconds. But I soon spotted the "object" referred to, about two to three hundred yards away down the valley to the east of our camp. Unquestionably, the figure in outline was exactly like a human being, walking upright and stopping occasionally to uproot or pull at some dwarf rhododendron bushes. It showed up dark against the snow and as far as I could make out, wore no clothes. Within the next minute or so it had moved into some thick scrub and was lost to view.

Tombazi had no time to take pictures, and the footprints he later examined were smaller than those normally made by a human foot. Perhaps he saw a yeti. Perhaps not. But regardless of what he saw, Tombazi's story was remembered whenever other travelers came back to Europe telling tales of strange creatures seen high in the Himalayas.

Then in 1951, mountaineer-explorer Eric Shipton actually took photographs of yeti footprints. His were the first photos to be brought out of Nepal.

Shipton's Photos

Shipton was climbing on the Menlung Glacier when he and his companions, Dr. Michael Ward and Sherpa guide Sen Tensing, discovered the prints. According to Ward, they followed the prints for "about a quarter to half a mile." Then they lost them in the

Explorer Eric Shipton and one of his photos of yeti footprints.

dirt and rocks beside the glacier.

Shipton took a number of photographs. Ward said the imprints "we photographed had the impression of five definite toes . . . the foot was very similar to that of a human being, except that of course it was broader." He said the prints were about twelve to fourteen inches long, and about six inches wide. He estimated that the creature weighed two hundred pounds or more.

Sen Tensing believed the prints were made by a yeti. Hence he remarked, "As no one has ever been here before, the yetis will be very frightened by our arrival.'' The other members of the mountaineering party were not as sure as Tensing that these were yeti tracks. But in a foreword to the book *Snowman and Company*, by Odette Tchernine, Shipton says, ''There could be no doubt whatever that a large creature had passed that way a very short time before, and that whatever it was it was not a human being, nor a bear, nor any species of monkey known to exist in Asia.'' Shipton added that in his widespread travels in the Himalayas he had never seen any comparable tracks.

Vladimir Tschernezkey, a zoologist, studied Shipton's photographs and concluded that the creature ''has extraordinarily thick . . . legs, legs that are much stronger than anything known in monkeys . . . and in any living or fossil human races.''

The yeti appear to be more apelike than human. But what about another hairy creature that has been seen in Asia? Is *it* human?

''Tibetans know their local animals and their distribution much better than any outsiders do . . . and would never for one moment confuse one with the other.''

Ivan T. Sanderson, author

''It is a popular delusion to imagine that countryfolk are universally and automatically experts on the animals that live on their doorsteps.''

John Napier, scientist

The Almas

While traveling in the mountains of southern Mongolia in 1963, Ivan Ivlov, a Russian doctor, saw a family of humanlike creatures called *Almas*. The family consisted of an adult male and female and a small offspring. Ivlov had heard local stories of these creatures, but had remained skeptical about their existence. Now he was able to actually observe them. From a distance of about half a mile, Ivlov watched through his field glasses until the family moved off and disappeared behind a jutting rock. The Mongol driver who accompanied him also saw the creatures.

As recently as 1974, a Mongol shepherd reported seeing an Almas in the Asgat Mountains. He described it as half human and half beast with reddish-black hair.

Information gleaned from the shepherd's account and that of sixteen other people who saw an Almas is quite consistent: No one has heard any of the creatures speak. They are most often seen at dawn or dusk in places far away from people, usually in

Above: Many times the yeti is described as resembling a primitive human being. Might some of our ancestors still be living in remote areas? Opposite page: Or might the yeti be some kind of mountain ape?

the summer when cattle are moved to distant pastures. Almas are similar in height to modern humans. They are shy, but unlike the Sasquatch, they are "apparently able to use tools," according to anthropologist Myra Shackley. In her book, *Still Living?* Shackley also says,

> "Almas seem to eke out a living . . . by hunting small mammals and eating wild plants, unassisted by fire although with shelter available in the form of caves. A crucial point, however, is that they do not appear to be *afraid* of fire, unlike all non-human species.
>
> "This very simple lifestyle and the nature of their appearance suggests strongly that Almas might represent the survival of a prehistoric way of life, and perhaps even of an earlier form of man."

"One of the strongest points in favor of the Yeti is that the Sherpas, though simple people, are neither damn fools nor subject to hallucinations."

John Masters, author

"There is no doubt that at high altitudes . . . human interpretation has at times been impaired to the extent of creating scenes and sounds that did not exist."

Odette Tchernine, author

Opposite page: Map of Eastern Tibet, China, and Mongolia, a geographic area with many Bigfoot sightings.

According to Francis Hitching in *The Mysterious World,* many Russians believe Almas may be descended from the primitive Neanderthals.

Professor Boris Porshnev, former director of the Modern History Department at Moscow Academy, regarded many of the Almas sightings as authentic, but he did not believe Almas to be human. Even if they were Neanderthals, he said, that did not make them human because Neanderthals were not human. "What kind of *man* is it that has no art, is hairy, and cannot speak? They are merely man-*like,* a separate group from men."

The Old Man of the Cave

In 1925, some Russian soldiers killed a wild, hairy humanlike creature that some people believed was an Almas. The soldiers were in the Pamir Mountains in southern Russia when they found footprints in the snow. They heard rustling sounds in a cave, and opened fire. Out of the cave staggered a creature covered with hair, but looking so human the men were baffled. According to Major General Topilsky, the officer in charge, "A doctor . . . swore 'it was not a human being,' although [his examination showed] the body was almost exactly like that of a man."

Hitching tells the rest of the story: "So man-like was the old creature . . . that the troops, unable to take it with them, buried it under a cache of stones. And thus the old man went to join what many Russians believe to be his forebears, the Neanderthals, in much the same way as he would have been buried some 40,000 years before."

Sasquatches, yetis, and Almas seem to be cousins to each other. Could there be still more relatives? Yes!

The Chinese Yeti

Ivan T. Sanderson thinks that "primitive and large creatures almost absolutely without any 'culture' in any sense of that term may live in eastern Tibet and China." These mysterious hairy creatures are called

USSR
MONGOLIA
Dzungaria
Altia
Inner Mongolia
CHINA
TIBET
Reports of Almas from this area

Right: A drawing of "the Chinese Wildman," believed to be a yeti. Opposite page: Many centuries ago, the continents of Asia and North America were connected by a vast "land bridge." Today all that remains is a swath of islands known as the Aleutian Archipelago. Might Bigfoot's ancestors have come to North America over the ancient land bridge?

by some authors Chinese Yeti. The Chinese refer to them as "wildmen."

In 1940, the shooting of a wildman was reported in China. Biologist Wang Zelin arrived at the scene shortly after it occurred. According to Myra Shackley, "Wang Zelin said the body was still supple and the stature was tall, approximately 6 feet 6 inches. The whole body was covered with a coat of thick greyish-red hair . . . The hair on the face was shorter. The face was narrow with deep-set eyes, while the cheek bones and lips jutted out. The scalp hair was roughly one foot long and untidy."

The local people told Wang that two such creatures had been in the area for over a month. They had noticed the wildmen had great strength, were "brisk in walking and could move as rapidly uphill as on the plain." They did not have a language and could only howl.

This Chinese version of the Abominable

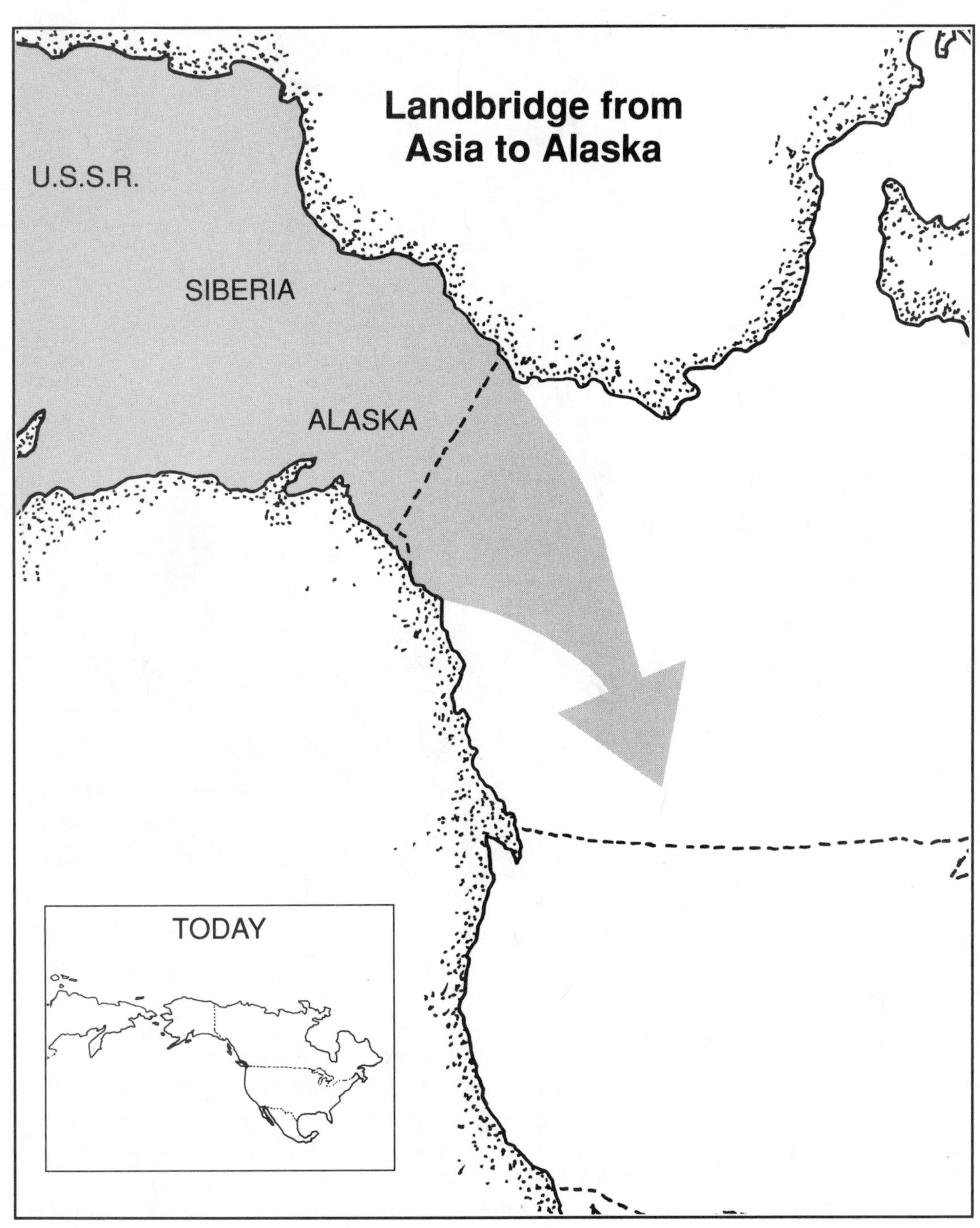
Landbridge from
Asia to Alaska
U.S.S.R.
SIBERIA
ALASKA
TODAY

The famous picture of the white Bigfoot seen near Lake Worth, Texas.

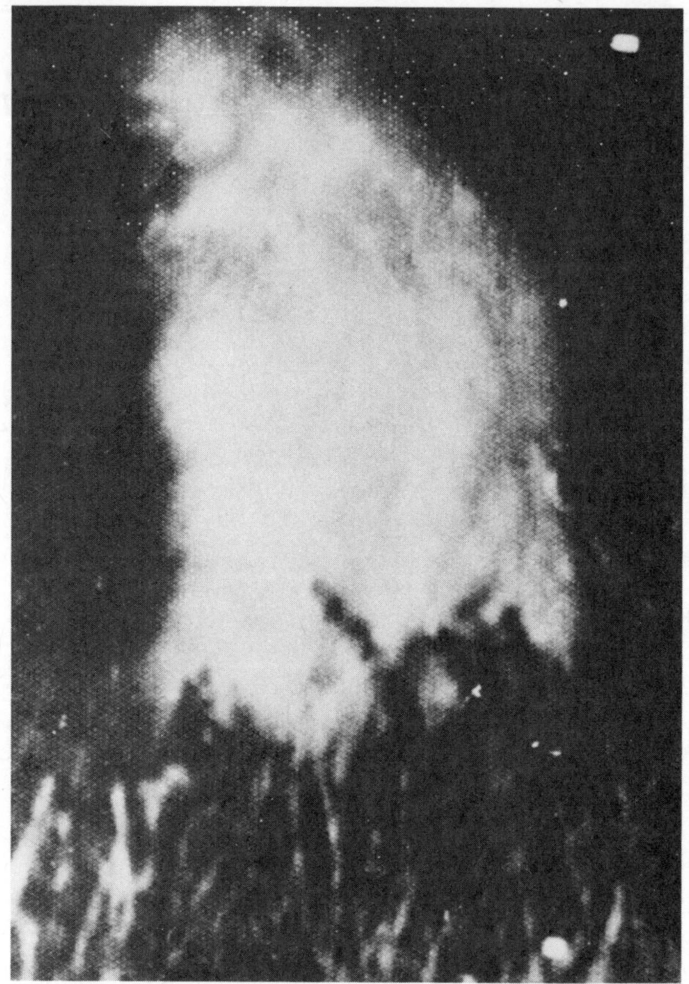

Snowman, or Bigfoot, also has teeth like a human's only larger. It can run as fast as a horse and swim in swift currents. In some cases the creature is said to have an obnoxious odor, just like Bigfoot!

How could these similar creatures have become distributed throughout such widely separated areas of the world? Scientists report that in prehistoric times the oceans receded, forming land bridges. One of these bridges extended from Asia to Alaska. If animals from China or Russia could cross over from the

Eastern to the Western hemisphere, perhaps Bigfoot's ancestors crossed too. Once in North America, they might have settled in the Pacific Northwest and other parts of the continent.

In 1969, a Bigfoot that smelled worse than a skunk was seen repeatedly in Lake Worth, Texas. Janet and Colin Bord in their *Bigfoot Casebook* report that, "On some nights in July the road through the nature reserve was packed with cars as the locals watched the famous beast cavort up and down a bluff." One time it hurled an old tire into the crowd, and the onlookers hastily leapt into their cars. The creature was described as being seven feet tall, white, and hairy. Observers said it "walked like a man." Allen Plaster, the owner of a local dress shop, even had a blurred black and white photograph of what he said was the Bigfoot.

The creature was apparently still around that fall. On November 7, Charles Buchanan was camping at Lake Worth. At two in the morning he was on top of his pickup truck asleep in his sleeping bag. Suddenly he was pulled off his truck and dropped to the ground. The smell, he said, was "overpowering." Thinking the beast might be looking for food, Buchanan grabbed a sack of leftover chicken and pushed it into Bigfoot's face. Bigfoot fastened his teeth into the sack, shuffled off into the lake, and swam away.

If so many of these wild creatures are on the loose, why haven't any been caught? Why can't anyone find concrete proof to back up the hundreds of stories from around the world?

"Two black shadows fell across [the yak herder's] path suddenly from one of the overhanging cliffs. . . . In a few minutes he found himself struggling with a monster. After the bloody duel, the villager extricated himself from the clutches of the creature with a superhuman effort. When he returned his fellow villagers found him swaying with giddiness and blood oozing from his eyes and nostrils."

G.N. Dutt, geologist and explorer

"That the Yeti would attack man without provocation is doubtful, and reports of encounters with one are in the main untrue."

Odette Tchernine, author

Four

On the Trail of Bigfoot

Hoping to find answers to the Bigfoot mystery, several people have mounted serious searches for the hairy monsters of the wilderness. One of these people, Sir Edmund Hillary, was a member of Eric Shipton's 1951 expedition in the Himalayas.

A Curious Hunter

Hillary was working in another valley when Shipton photographed the so-called yeti footprints. When Hillary saw the photos he became intensely curious. He couldn't put them out of his mind.

When he returned to the Himalayas two years later, he and Tensing Norgay, his Sherpa guide, made history by becoming the first persons ever to reach the top of Mount Everest. During their climb they found mysterious tracks in the snow. But the footprints didn't frighten Hillary. He vowed that the next time he was in the Himalayas he would hunt for the Abominable Snowman.

And in 1960 he did. Hillary's primary purpose on this expedition was to learn how humans could adjust to climbing in high altitudes with little oxygen. But he also took along equipment to photograph any

Sir Edmund Hillary and Tensing Norgay, the first men to climb to the top of Mt. Everest.

Sir Edmund Hillary's expedition equipment. Hillary is second from right. Second from left. Marlin Perkins, long-time television host of *Wild Kingdom,* holds a gun intended to disable but not kill or injure a Bigfoot or dangerous animal.

snowman he might find. In addition to cameras, Hillary carried tranquilizing guns so he could stun the creature and examine it. Because the religion of Nepal forbids the killing of animals, Hillary never thought of bringing back a dead specimen. Since they had no means of taking a live one back down the mountain, he would have to examine it there and let it go. Hillary was cautious, though. He took along tear gas in case a snowman attacked him or any of the other climbers.

While he prepared for his expedition, Hillary listened carefully to the natives' stories. They told about whistling noises stabbing through the darkness on winter nights; about huge footprints being found near villages; and about religious men called *lamas* seeing yetis near their monastery buildings.

Hillary and his climbers listened to advice, too. They were told that the clothes they wore were so brightly colored the yetis would spot them easily and stay away. They changed their gear.

They started off with high hopes. They moved slowly through the snow-covered mountains and

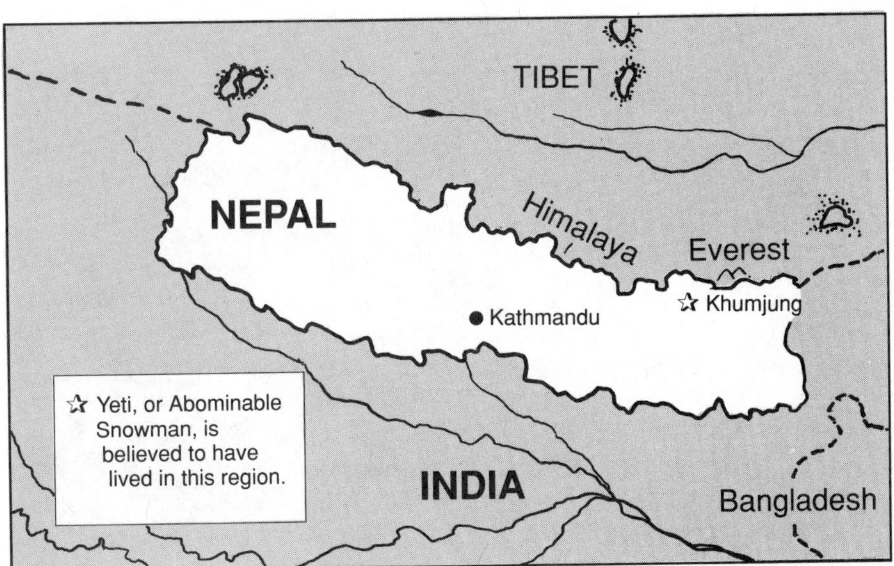

Map shows the location of the village where Hillary's team was entrusted with the yeti scalp.

stopped in every village seeking information. In one village they were told a yeti had been seen recently. Sure enough, Hillary's team found footprints in the snow! The prints looked like they'd been made by a large, barefooted human. The team photographed the prints and made plaster casts for later study.

When the expedition arrived in the village of Khumjung, Hillary was shown a scalp said to be that of a yeti. The thick skin was covered with black and red hair, and it was dome-shaped. Hillary convinced the villagers to let him take it to a university to have it examined by experts. Because he promised to return the scalp, they agreed. The natives said the gods would be angry if the scalp was not returned. They made Hillary take a Sherpa guide along to be sure he kept his promise.

Scientists in Chicago who examined the "scalp" said it was really the hide of the serow, a wild goat antelope. Scientists in Paris said it was from a bear. Both groups of scientists agreed that it probably came from an animal that had died hundreds of years ago.

John Napier thought the scalp given to Hillary may

An officer of Nepal holds the scalp long believed to have belonged to a yeti.

not have been the original. Perhaps the villagers had made a replica of the real one and given the copy to Hillary. Napier said, "A 'real' scalp is said to exist in the monastery at Rongbuk in Tibet."

Hillary returned the scalp, but the villagers in Khumjung refused to believe what the scientists had said. To them it would always be a yeti scalp.

"The truth is that scientists are simply not interested in investigating problems for which there is not sufficient evidence to justify launching an expensive time- and energy-consuming project."

John Napier, scientist

Explaining the Footprints

Desmond Doig, a journalist and mountaineer who accompanied Hillary on his expedition, offers an explanation for the footprints. He says that yetis very likely are blue bears that have come into Nepal from neighboring Tibet. "Tibetans insist that the blue bear walks a great deal on its hind legs," he adds.

"There is now vastly more evidence to prove that he does exist, than there is to prove that he does not."

Ralph Izzard, reporter

Napier says that yetis and blue bears do apparently live in the same area. But he is not ready to accept that all the prints found are made by blue bears because he contends that blue bears do *not* walk on their hind legs. "They may briefly stand upright on two legs, but they certainly never walk on them." So, according to Napier, the mysterious beast is not a bear.

That the prints may have been made by the Alpine chough (pronounced *chuff*), a common bird in the Himalayas, is another possibility. This bird sometimes hops along breast-deep in the snow, leaving tracks that look like human footprints! Furthermore, the choughs have a high-pitched, mewing call which could be mistaken for the yelping of a yeti. The "yeti call" is heard more often than the animal or its tracks are seen.

Is the yeti, then, nothing but a bird?

Or did a human being make those tracks? Religious pilgrims wander the heights of the Himalayas. These people are seemingly unaffected by the cold. They walk barefooted and have been known to sleep in the snow with no shelter. Perhaps their tracks have been mistakenly attributed to the yeti.

Napier insists that "not all prints seen over the

years by reputable observers can be explained away.'' George Schaller, an ethologist (one who studies animal behavior), is convinced that ''an animal unknown to science'' lives in the Himalayan uplands.

Is this unknown animal also roaming the woods in North America? A Swiss-born adventurer wanted to find out.

Opposite page: Himalayan blue bear. Above: Serow goats. These two animals look very different from one another, yet both have been mistaken for yetis.

A Lifelong Searcher

In December 1953, René Dahinden was working on a farm in Canada. One day he heard a radio account of an expedition being formed to search for yetis in the Himalaya Mountains. Dahinden was fascinated.

''Now wouldn't that be something, to be on the hunt for that thing?'' he asked the farmer. The farmer told Dahinden that he needn't go that far if he wanted to search for a creature like the yeti. He could find big hairy monsters in western Canada.

Throughout the winter the farmer told Dahinden

"When we start to put into operation the full-scale searching of a fully funded team, then I feel that we will at last come to grips with the Bigfeet and, with our efforts, pierce the shadows of one of the most extraordinary mysteries of our time."

Peter Byrne, explorer

"The Yeti is more likely to be met in a chance encounter round, say, a rock, than by an organized search."

Ralph Izzard, reporter

Sasquatch stories he had heard while working on the west coast some years before. His descriptions were similar to those of the yeti. Dahinden listened and made plans.

The following spring Dahinden went to work in a sawmill in British Columbia. He spent hours in the Vancouver public library reading about Sasquatches and studying newspaper accounts of sightings. The general attitude of the books and articles he read was that Bigfoot is an Indian legend, nothing more.

But Dahinden persisted and dug deeper. By 1956 he'd found enough material to convince himself that Bigfoot was something worth seriously pursuing. He started keeping a file of sightings. "I really wasn't equipped at that time to evaluate what I was reading and hearing," he said. "I accepted—probably because I wanted to—the word of those people who said the thing existed and who pointed to stories that had never been investigated." Author Don Hunter says Dahinden began his quest as much for fun as for anything else, but his attitude changed as he heard more and more stories. He began to carefully analyze each one. Some he rejected altogether because he thought the people were unreliable or were looking for publicity. Others were obviously lies or were cases in which people had simply mistaken an ordinary animal for a Bigfoot. But many of the stories, Dahinden believed, were true.

For example, Dahinden listened to Albert Ostman's experience with the family of Sasquatches. He says Ostman told his story many times with never a shift of detail. Dahinden believed Ostman was definitely telling the truth.

Because of Dahinden's willingness to listen, many people who were reluctant to tell their Bigfoot stories came forward and did so. Hunter says, "The hundreds of reports that are now on record are there largely through Dahinden's persistent searching." His catalog of names, dates, and sightings form a strong case for the existence of the Sasquatch.

Dahinden himself has come to no conclusions, but proving or disproving the existence of the Sasquatch has become a lifelong interest. He is often called upon to make a judgment on the validity of Bigfoot stories as they come in.

A Professional Stalker

Another dedicated Bigfoot hunter is Peter Byrne of Mount Hood, Oregon. In his book, *The Search for Bigfoot*, Byrne says he recalls his father "telling me bedside stories . . . years ago, and spinning yarns about the swirling mists of the high Himalayas and the giant hairy men that inhabited those inhospitable regions." In 1956, Byrne and a group of men went on an expedition to "find the Yeti." They found one set of footprints, a scalp that was said to be from a yeti, and a mummified hand from what might have

Above: The Slick Expedition relaxes after a long day of Bigfoot hunting. Right: Explorer Peter Byrne sets up a telescope to better seek Bigfoot.

Left: A trail of Bigfoot prints in the Blue Creek Mountains in northern California. Right: Bigfoot seeker René Dahinden measures one of the Blue Creek Mountain prints—it's fifteen inches long!

been a yeti or a human—no one has ever decided which. The men searched the cold, windy mountains for three years until a Sherpa brought them a crumpled letter from the United States. It was from Tom Slick, the Texas millionaire who had financed the trip. Slick asked them to come back to the U.S. and take over an expedition searching for Bigfoot. Byrne's party didn't hesitate. They started packing immediately.

The group arrived in Willow Creek, California, and organized what Byrne called "a systematic and sensible approach" to finding Bigfoot. Dahinden joined Slick's expedition for a while, but he didn't stay long. He didn't like Slick's method of promising extra money to anyone who could catch a Sasquatch. Bob Titmus, a taxidermist, was so eager to get the reward money he put out trays of food to attract a Bigfoot. He stuck food under bushes, on logs, and in trees. Wherever he put bait, he set up a camera aimed at it. Dahinden left in disgust when the expedition, in Hunter's words, "turned out to be a disorganized gallop through the woods."

By 1960 the Slick expedition had found a total of twelve sets of footprints. Byrne said, "We did not see a Bigfoot."

When Tom Slick was killed in an airplane crash, the financial support for the expedition ended. Byrne went back to Nepal and became involved in big game hunting. He later returned to the United States to make a full-time profession of Sasquatch research after he received funding from the Academy of Applied Science in Boston. Byrne used the grant to set up the Bigfoot Information Center in Hood River, Oregon. The Center has since been closed, but Byrne's records of its ten years of research are available to anyone interested in learning about Bigfoot.

A Scientist Becomes Interested

So far, only people who had little scientific training in identifying animals had tried to find a Bigfoot.

"Bring me a specimen, or a good skeleton, then I'll believe something is there. Bring me *hard* evidence."

Richard W. Thorington Jr., curator of the National Museum of Natural History

"Ask any game warden, real woodsman or professional animal collector if he has ever found the dead body or even a bone of *any* wild animal—except along roads of course, or if killed by man. I never have, in forty years on five continents!"

Ivan T. Sanderson, scientist

Then, in August 1967, hundreds of new Bigfoot tracks were found in British Columbia, Canada. Heavy pieces of equipment had been strewn about, and the area was surrounded by clear prints. Finally Don Abbott, an anthropologist from the British Columbia Provincial Museum, came to examine the prints. This was the first time on record that any authoritative institution had become interested in Sasquatch activity.

Before Abbott could complete a careful investigation, however, carloads of curious people came to the scene. They stomped in and around the footprints, comparing the size with their own feet. The evidence was destroyed.

Abbott was impressed by the few prints that had not been ruined. He wanted to preserve some of them by using a fixative which hardened the ground, allowing the actual footprint to be lifted out for further study. Before he could do this, however, a road-grader operator, anxious to see the road smooth again, covered the prints.

It appeared the first scientific investigation of a Bigfoot was going to fall through. But something else happened that year that gave scientists more evidence to examine.

A Starring Role!

Roger Patterson, a rodeo cowboy, filmed a Bigfoot! Patterson had been searching for Bigfoot off and on for six years. In October 1967, Patterson and a partner, Bob Gimlin, rode into the Bluff Creek area on horseback. About twenty-five miles into this rugged mountain country they came around a bend in the creek and their horses suddenly reared. On the other side of the creek about eighty to a hundred feet away, a large, hairy creature stood erect. According to author Kenneth Wylie's account, Patterson rushed "on foot across the little stream, stumbling in the soft sand,

Three frames from Roger Patterson's famous film of Bigfoot. Some viewers argue that the creature must be a human in some kind of gorilla suit. Others insist that everything about the creature was so realistic that it must be a genuine Bigfoot.

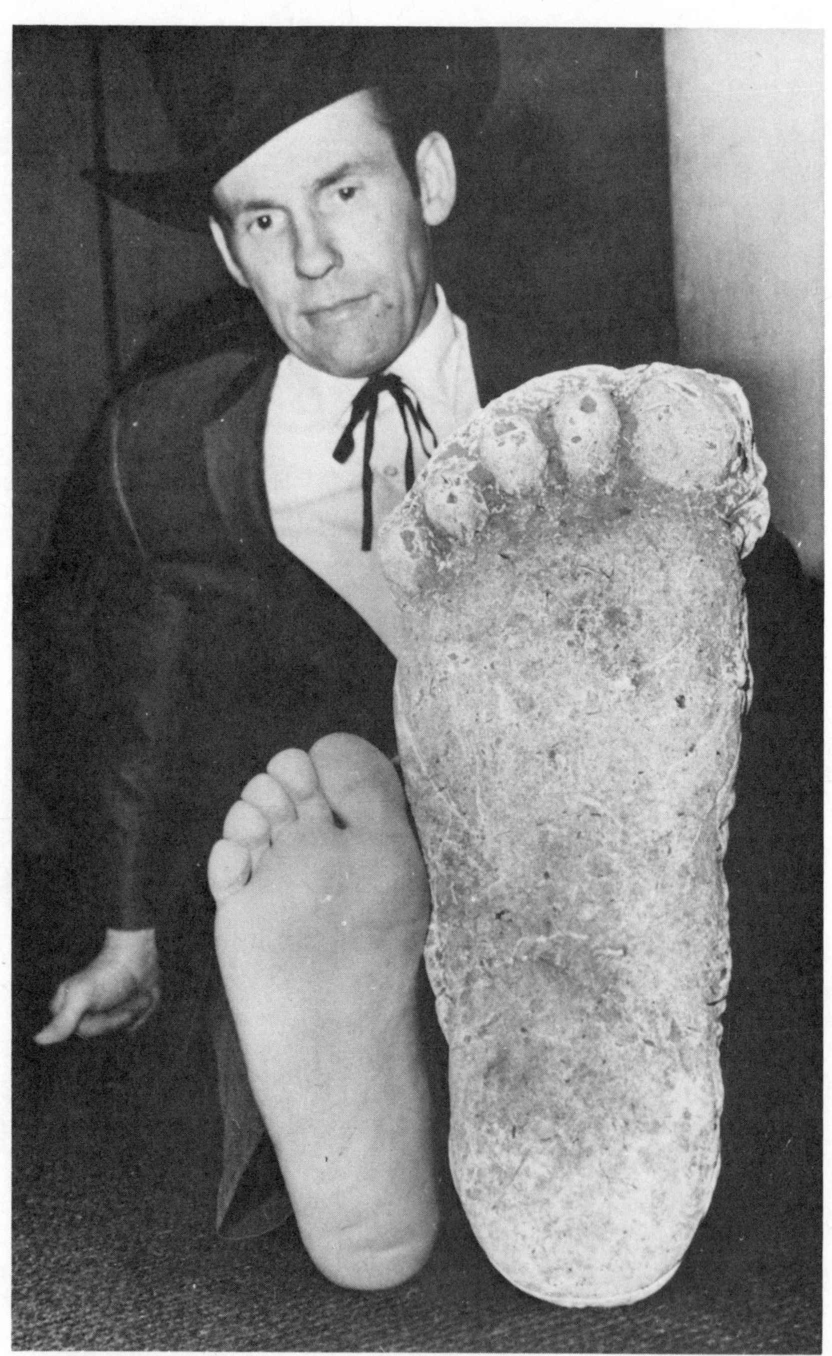

Photographer Roger Patterson compares his foot to a plaster cast of one of the footprints left at the scene of his film.

camera in hand, to catch this strange thing on film.''

Patterson regained his footing and the result was twenty-four feet of sixteen millimeter color movie film of what Patterson claimed was a Sasquatch walking in the woods. The creature even paused once to look back at the men.

Patterson said, ''Its head was very human, though considerably more slanted, and with a large forehead and wide nostrils. Its arms hung almost to its knees when it walked. Its hair was two to four inches long, brown underneath, lighter at the top, and covering the entire body except for the face. And it was female; it had big, pendulous breasts.'' He and Gimlin estimated its height at close to seven feet. From impressions left on the sandbar, they guessed its weight at about 350 pounds.

Patterson showed his film to groups of scientists. Some of them immediately said the creature in the film was a fake. Others kept a more open mind, but had questions.

Frank Beebe, of the British Columbia Provincial Museum, wondered why the creature had a bony crest on its skull, like a male gorilla, but no pot belly like gorillas and orangutans have.

Scientist William Montagna, an expert on primates and primate skin, pointed out that the breasts of human females are not covered with hair, but that Patterson's

Below: Hollywood technicians at Lucasfilm turn an ordinary elephant into a space creature for the film *Star Wars.* If they can do this, could other technicians make a Bigfoot?

A makeup person straightens Chewbacca's fur before filming a scene for *Star Wars*.

Bigfoot had hairy breasts. Montagna therefore concluded that it was not human. Peter Byrne added that apes do not have breasts, so it couldn't have been an ape.

In an effort to convince the skeptics that the creature was real, Patterson and Gimlin took the film to technicians at Universal Studios in Hollywood. Technicians manufacture monsters like King Kong for the movies. They, if anyone, should know if the Bigfoot had been faked. They examined the film. Patterson then asked them if it would have been possible to make such a creature. They replied: "We could try. But we would have to create a completely new system of artificial muscles and find an actor who could be trained to walk like that. It might be done, but we would have to say that it would be almost impossible."

René Dahinden viewed the film too. He felt that it was solid evidence of Bigfoot's existence. He com-

Top: This photo was first said to be a genuine picture of a Bigfoot taking a shower. Later it was shown to be a fraud. Middle: A gorilla suit used in a Bigfoot hoax. Bottom: Roger Patterson's Bigfoot. There has never been any proof that this Bigfoot is not real.

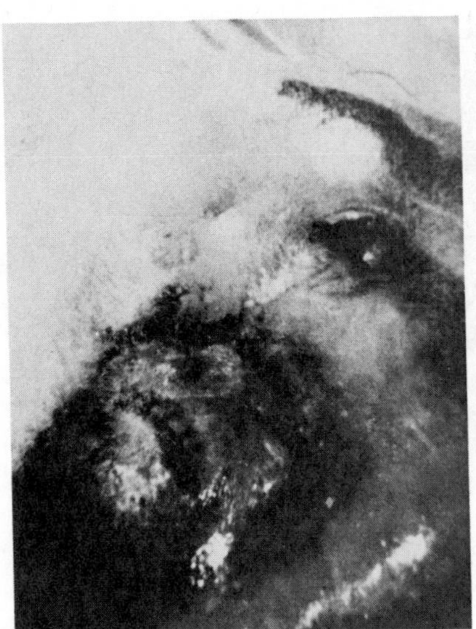

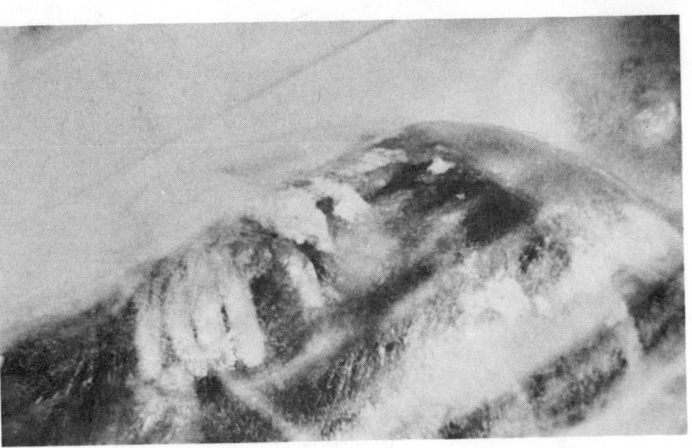

Two of the only existing photos of the Minnesota Iceman. Above: His mouth and perhaps an eye are visible through the ice. Above right: The Iceman's hand can be seen.

mented that in the newspaper stories which followed the incident, there was "a remarkable scarcity of the comic tone" that had always characterized reporting about Sasquatch. Dahinden thought a scientific investigation might finally take place. He was delighted.

But then Don Abbott stated, "Like most scientists . . . I'm not ready to put my reputation on the line until something concrete shows up—something like bones or a skull."

European Expert

Dahinden was discouraged that Abbott wouldn't pursue an investigation. But he did not let the matter rest. He took the film to Dr. Don Grieve in Europe. Grieve was an expert in biomechanics, or how bodies and muscles move. He said that if the film was taken at sixteen or eighteen frames per second, then the combination of the creature's body movements were "not compatible with those of any normal human gait." But if the camera was used at twenty-four frames per second, then "all movements do fit together into a humanlike combination." Unfortunately Patterson didn't know what speed his camera had been set for.

So what did Patterson film?

Was it a living monster or someone dressed up

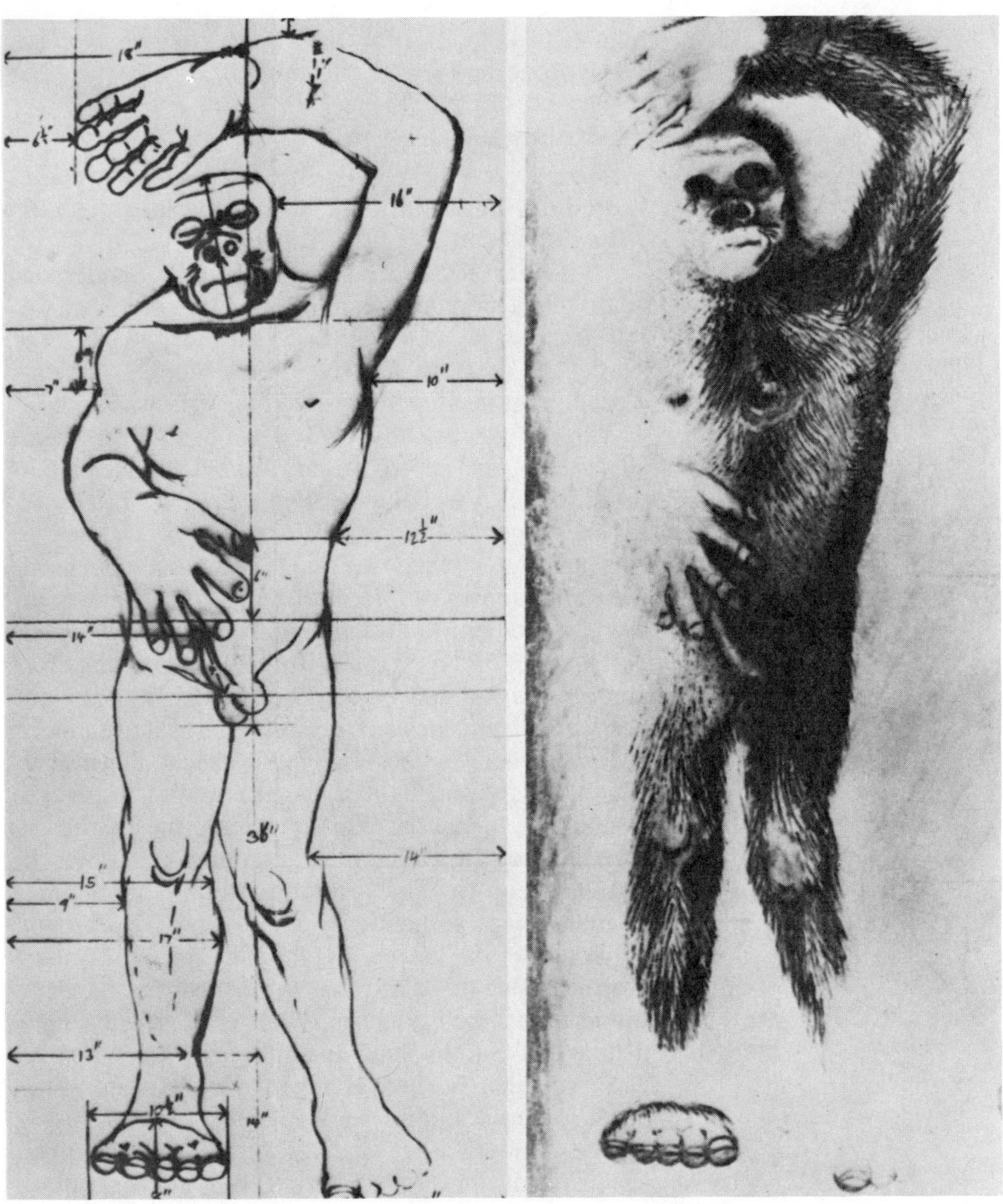

Ivan Sanderson's sketches of the Minnesota Iceman. Did this creature actually exist, or was it only a hoax? If it was real, could it have been a Bigfoot?

"The creature known as the 'Ice Man' . . . could indeed have been a young Bigfoot. I personally believe that it was."

Peter Byrne, explorer

"From a journalistic point of view, the Iceman was a great story while it lasted, but I believe it has only served further to degrade the Bigfoot legend."

John Napier, scientist

in a fur suit?

No one has solved the mystery.

The Minnesota Iceman

Like Don Abbott, other scientists wanted evidence more solid than a film. And the next year, something *frozen* solid turned up in Minnesota.

In December 1968, scientist Ivan T. Sanderson heard that a strange, humanlike creature had been on traveling display in the United States for the past two years. The creature was frozen in a block of ice enclosed in an insulated coffin. The coffin was kept in a refrigerated truck in which it had been taken from city to city and shown at carnivals. The truck with its "iceman" was being kept on a farm in Minnesota for the winter.

Sanderson and Belgian zoologist Bernard Heuvelmans went to view the monster. They spent two days studying the creature in its coffin. They noted that the feet of the creature were adapted neither for climbing (as an ape's would be) nor for walking on two feet. The hands were neither apelike nor human, but somewhere in between. The hair had alternating bands of dark and light, a pattern similar to that of a squirrel's fur. It was like no creature they had ever seen before. Heuvelmans was convinced it was a genuine deep-frozen Neanderthal. Sanderson, too, thought it was authentic.

Because of the lack of space in the truck, photographing this discovery was difficult, so Sanderson made detailed sketches. Then he informed scientists at the Smithsonian Institution in Washington, D.C., of what he and Heuvelmans had seen. The Smithsonian scientists were interested in the possibility of finding a new species, but the iceman mysteriously disappeared before the scientists could examine it!

Frank D. Hansen, the man who displayed the creature, said the owner had come and taken the

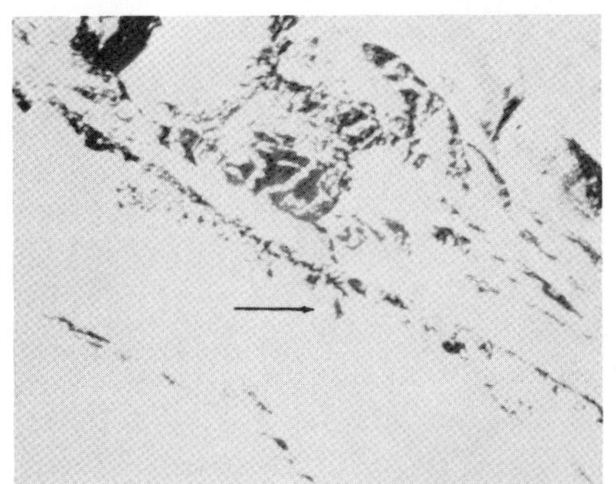

In March 1986, in the Himalayas, an explorer named Anthony Wooldridge sighted what he thought was a yeti a great distance away. He excitedly took photos. For a time the scientific community thought proof of a living Bigfoot might finally have been found. Sadly, careful scientific analysis of the photos indicated that Wooldridge's eyes—and camera—had played a trick on him. Bigfoot turned out to be a rock!

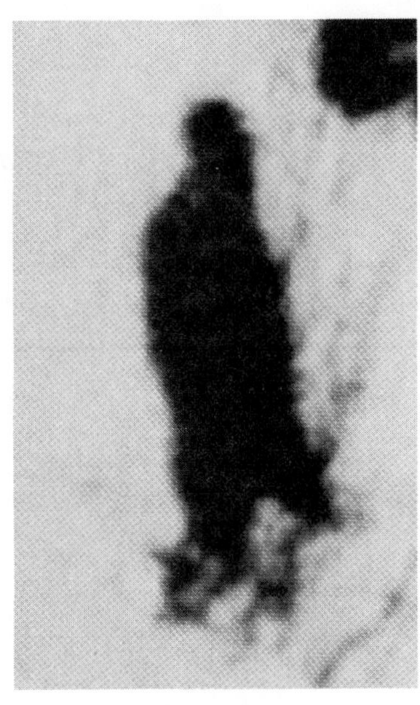

specimen away. He said the owner was a West Coast millionaire connected with the movies. If Hansen knew his name, he was not revealing it.

Three separate organizations came forward to claim they had made the model of the iceman for Hansen to show at carnivals. No proof indicated that any of them were telling the truth. The iceman was never found.

John Napier commented that, "If it is not made of latex rubber and expanded polystyrene it represents a living species; there are no alternatives."

Hansen never claimed that his exhibit was anything but a mystery. That's what it was. And still is.

Five

Real or Hoax?

Around the world, sightings of Bigfoot are still being reported. One sighting took place on March 18, 1987, near Fellers Heights in British Columbia, Canada. A seven-man oil crew was working outdoors in the frozen wilderness when four of the men saw something skirting the worksite. They described it as a seven-foot, four hundred-pound monster. It was "more like a man than an animal," Myles Jack, one of the workers, said. "But it was a real mover. It was really fluid in the way it moved." The creature crouched for a time and watched the men. Then it peered at them through the trees as it circled the worksite. "It was like we were on his territory and he was checking us out," said Jack. "He seemed really curious."

Jack yelled at his pal Bryan Mestdagh who turned around and saw the hulking figure. "I've seen a documentary on the Sasquatch and I'd have to say what we saw was identical," Mestdagh said. He added that the men had not been drinking when they saw the creature. "There was no drink or anything else. We saw what we saw."

Mestdagh has worked in the northern forests for

Outdoor workers in wooded areas are frequently the people who sight Bigfoot.

Bigfoot seeker René Dahinden believes that eventually unequivocal evidence of Bigfoot's existence will be found. Here, Dahinden (left) interviews Fred Beek, who claims he shot a Bigfoot in Washington in 1924.

more than a decade. He told a reporter for *The Province* newspaper that the creature could not possibly have been a bear. "Its legs were too long and it moved too quick . . . for it to be a bear." The footprints were still visible when Ann Rees, a *Province* staff reporter, visited the isolated clearing. Rees wrote, "It's being dubbed the best Sasquatch sighting in almost a decade."

René Dahinden was called in to investigate. He was impressed with a print which seemed to indicate the creature had indeed been crouching while watching the workers. Dahinden ruled out the possibility of pranksters. "Planting footprints in the ground six feet apart in a foot and one-half of snow with no disturbance between the prints is just not that simple," he said. "Besides, it wouldn't have the weight that these prints seem to indicate."

A Hoax?

Sightings like these have encouraged Dahinden not to give up hope in his quest for the Sasquatch. He believes it might be real. But others are not so sure. Perhaps it is, after all, only a joke. The stories could be lies. The footprints could be fakes.

But if a person is going to tell a story which he or she imagined, wouldn't that person make the story as interesting as possible? Why just tell about a hairy giant who walked away and did *nothing*? Why have it walking on only two feet? Why not six or eight? Why not make the story better by saying the monster had green hair and purple horns and wore a ballet skirt?

Peter Byrne thinks that because so many people in widely separated places and times describe essentially the same creature, their stories are all the more believable. He says, "All of the stories have a

Bigfoot explorer Peter Byrne holds the cast of a sixteen-inch Bigfoot footprint.

Would anyone go to the trouble of learning human anatomy just to make a convincing Bigfoot footprint?

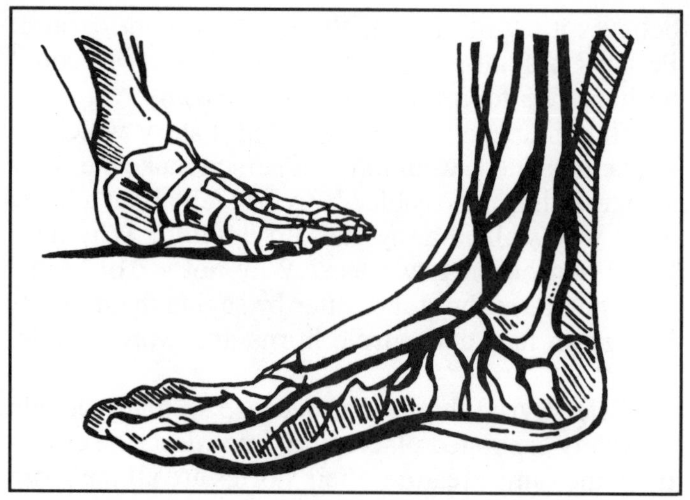

sameness, a repetition that, were the subject matter not so interesting, would make them dull reading indeed.''

And what about the footprints?

Physical anthropologist Grover S. Krantz of Washington State University has examined over sixty casts and photographs of footprints said to have been made by Sasquatches. If the footprints were faked, according to Krantz, the person playing the trick would have had to carry hundreds of pounds of weight to make the imprints as deep as they were. Also, ''independent toe movements as noticed in some tracks would require a special device to accomplish.'' The trickster would have had to wear the device or carry it over miles of rugged terrain. He or she could not have left any human tracks uncovered.

To make a device that would fool scientists, a person would have to know the anatomy of the human foot. Especially in the case of the *crippled* Bigfoot.

In November 1969, some prints that were apparently made by a Bigfoot were found near Bossburg, Washington. The prints showed that the right foot was deformed. The third toe was either badly twisted over or was missing. The whole foot curved outwards and

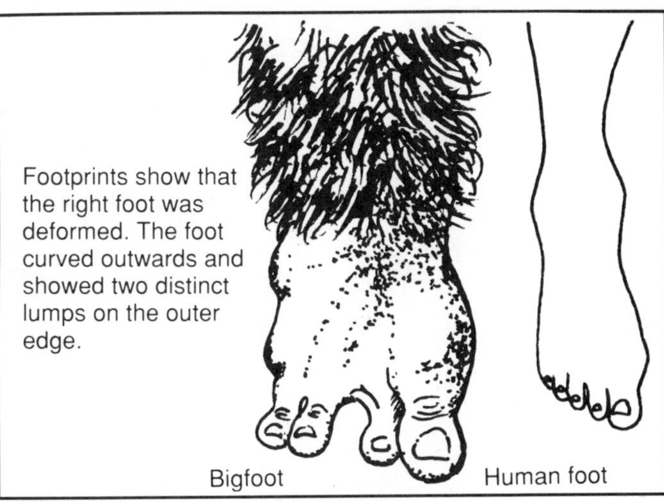

If the Bossburg footprint was a fake, it was remarkable. Sophisticated knowledge of anatomy would have been necessary.

showed two distinct lumps on the outer edge. Scientists were amazed. They felt the footprints were either real, or whoever had made the tracks knew just how a creature handicapped in this way would move so as to leave such a print. Scientists still don't know what made the Bossburg prints.

Maybe Bigfoot Is Real

Krantz says that, as a result of the knowledge gained from the study of Bigfoot tracks, "Even if none of the hundreds of *sightings* had ever occurred, we would still be forced to conclude that a giant bipedal [two-footed] primate does indeed inhabit the forests of the Pacific Northwest."

Is Krantz right?

He could be. Certainly the creatures could stay hidden. Peter Byrne cites an example of Japanese soldiers who lived undiscovered for many years in desolate areas. They went into hiding when World War II ended and were found years later living off the land. One survived alone for over twenty-five years. He did not know the war had ended. He was discovered on the island of Guam which has an area of 209 square miles and a population of 87,000 people.

"A man who is too much like an animal and not enough like a man is all wrong. He is both scary and disgusting. And I guess that is what 'abominable' means."

Joseph Wood Krutch, author

"Tomorrow we may know one of our other relatives: the abominable snowman, for instance, who is surely a shy and gentle great ape."

Bernard Heuvelmans, zoologist

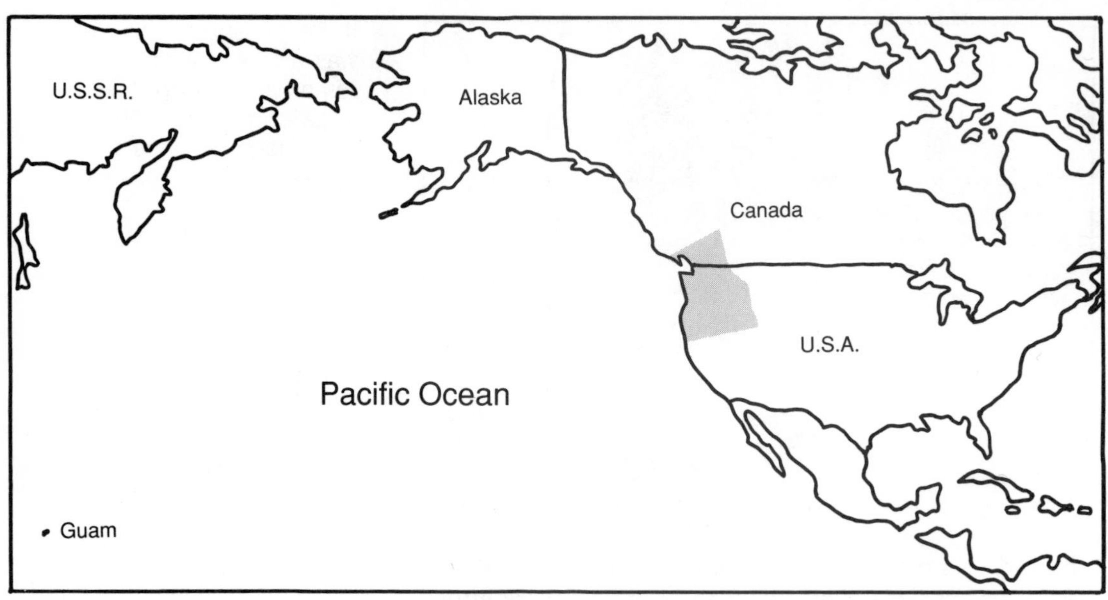

A Japanese soldier stayed hidden on the island of Guam for twenty-five years. The Pacific Northwest is much larger than Guam. Therefore wouldn't it be easy for a Bigfoot to stay hidden from the prying eyes of hunters?

The Bigfoot area of the Pacific Northwest is 125,000 square miles—*much* larger than Guam!

Byrne comments: "The Bigfeet, if they do indeed live in this huge range of forested mountains, are obviously not sitting around waiting to be discovered." In fact, they are constantly on the move. Byrne thinks that Bigfoot does not want to be found.

But another question arises: Even if living Bigfeet can avoid human contact most of their lives, why aren't they found when they die?

Buried Sasquatches?

Byrne says that perhaps Sasquatches "bury their dead and bury them deep." He tells of a man who swore he watched three Bigfeet burying a fourth. After digging a deep hole, using only their hands as tools, they placed the body in the hole and covered it with earth. Then they rolled huge boulders onto the grave. This grave has never been found.

No fossils have been found of Bigfoot either. Fossils would be convincing evidence for scientists. But Byrne says that in wet acid soils, bones disap-

The dense forest and rugged mountains of the Pacific Northwest are a perfect hiding place for the elusive Bigfoot. A road surveyor saw a Bigfoot carrying a fish at this scene, the Sheckamus River in British Columbia.

pear without fossilizing. The soil in the Pacific Northwest is wet and acidic.

In addition, a natural disposal system operates in Bigfoot's North American area. It consists of crows and ravens, buzzards, and other meat-eating birds. Byrne lists other members of this disposal squad: "coyotes, wolves, foxes, various rodents, and porcupines. They are often led by the black bear. Everything is eaten, even the antlers of big buck deer."

The absence of bone or fossil evidence is frustrating. Without it there is no proof. Scientists need a skeleton, such as the one author Alan Landsburg saw in a college museum in Dublin, Ireland. In his

Crows and other scavengers may be the reason no remains of a Bigfoot have ever been found.

book *In Search of Myths and Monsters*, he says the skeleton was of an eight-foot-six-inch tall human. He explains, "Science would never have accepted the possibility of eight-foot men, were it not for their skeletons and graves."

Landsburg wonders if giant humans could have mated with huge apes millions of years ago and produced a new breed. Could this new breed still be living in seclusion except for the rare moments when one is seen in high mountain passes or beside a quiet stream?

Another possibility, says Landsburg, is that when the huge apes came in contact with evolving humans, they wandered off into high country where they wouldn't have to compete for food and other necessities. Perhaps they still exist but are becoming fewer each year as more roads are built and more people fish and camp in the wilderness.

"No," says journalist John Green. "There are hundreds of thousands of square miles of suitable habitat for it in which pressure from humans is minimal . . . the Sasquatch population must surely number at least in the thousands."

Still, no specimen, dead or alive, has been brought out of the dark, silent forest.

Perhaps Bigfoot is not an earth creature at all. Some people think Bigfoot is a visitor from another planet. This photo of a reported flying saucer was taken in Oregon, an area of many Bigfoot sightings.

Why?

Maybe the Sasquatch doesn't live in the forest after all. Maybe it doesn't even live on Earth. A story told by authors B. Ann Slate and Alan R. Berry suggests this possibility.

Not of This Earth

They say it happened on a hilltop in Pennsylvania. One night, fifteen people gathered when they saw an enormous glowing ball descend from the sky and slowly come to rest on the grass. The object was dome-shaped and made a noise "like a rotary lawn mower." As the crowd watched, two figures emerged from the shadows. In the light from this unidentified

“Our Bigfoot is marvelously elusive. No one seems to be able to agree exactly which is the best place to look.”

Kenneth Wylie, author

“It is interesting that the reports of these creatures come only from those environments that could actually support such a form of life. Most of the habitats are in or near mountain forests.”

Stephen Rudley, author

flying object, the people saw two tall, hairy monsters with large, shining yellow-green eyes.

A man in the crowd fired his rifle at the giants and apparently hit one. It made a whining sound as if to warn its companion. At that instant the UFO vanished, leaving only a low-lying brightness that lingered at the site.

A state trooper who came to investigate the incident said he noticed that when he moved along the fence at the outer edge of the woods, “something large concealed in the trees” moved along with him.

No wounded monster was ever found. No one knows where the monsters went. Were they Bigfoot creatures just visiting Earth? Slate and Berry ask: “Is it possible that [Bigfoot] is, and always has been a tool of . . . the UFO intelligences?”

John Green doesn’t think so. “As to linking the Sasquatch with visitors from outer space, I see no need to do so. It is understandable . . . that when people report seeing an animal that science insists does not exist on Earth, it should be suggested that it comes from somewhere else.” But where?

If Sasquatches do come from outer space, then they may not be human. But even if they aren’t, should people with rifles be shooting at them? This question has concerned some Sasquatch seekers.

Capture or Kill?

Naturalist Frank Beebe says, “If I were out in the mountains and I saw a thing like this one [a Sasquatch], I wouldn’t shoot it. I’d be too afraid of how human it would look under that fur.” Scientist Jon E. Beckjord of Seattle agrees: “Because these reports feature *hairy* bodies, and not hairless bodies, we have persons who feel this is license to shoot first and ask questions afterward. I deplore this form of . . . arrogance.”

If killing a Sasquatch would be like killing a human being, then capturing one is the only way to

The mystery of Bigfoot intrigues many people. Some want to capture one so that it can be studied more closely. Here Peter Byrne prepares some Bigfoot scent, a special "perfume" designed to attract a Bigfoot. This is a technique used by many hunters.

get a specimen for scientific study. But Grover S. Krantz cautions anyone who attempts to do this. "This is not only probably futile, but it may be extremely dangerous. Various methods have been proposed, including some elaborate traps, but the tranquilizing dart rifle is the most commonly expressed idea." Even this presents problems. States Krantz, "Too much, or the wrong drug, or used on too small a specimen, all could lead to the death of the quarry. In this case, a regular rifle would have done a cleaner, less painful job." Green adds, "In reaction to the above recommendation, I have already been asked, 'Isn't it possible to get such proof without committing murder?' To this I can only respond, 'Isn't it possible to eat a hamburger without being a cannibal?' The crux of this exchange is whether the Sasquatch is human in any sense of the word, and the answer is no.''

Jon E. Beckjord argues that there's no reason not to kill ''an alleged new species of fish, or snake, or gopher.'' But when it comes to Sasquatches, he says that is another matter. ''We do not know if the Sasquatches are . . . a new race of humans, evolved gorillas, agents of extraterrestrial forces, or simply the figment of observers' imaginations. We do not know.

''And since we do not know, let us be careful,'' he adds. "We must tread softly when using the powers of life and death in the name of 'science'."

''It really is quite difficult to imagine how a single species could have hidden itself for so long.''

Daniel Cohen, author

''The yeti would have little trouble escaping detection in the steep valleys [of the Arun River in Nepal]. The dense vegetation presents a nearly impenetrable wall. . . . It would have been possible for a large mammal to hide within fifty yards of me and remain unnoticed.''

E.W. Cronin Jr., zoologist

Even more impressive evidence than footprints must be found before skeptics will be convinced that Bigfoot is real. Here Bob Gimlin and Roger Patterson examine casts made of footprints left at the site of Patterson's film. Not everyone is convinced they are genuine.

Conclusion

A Mystery To Solve

If a real creature is responsible for the many eyewitness reports of monsters roaming the wilderness, then according to John Green, "We are dealing with something that walks upright like a human but is entirely covered with hair and is usually much larger than a human." It is more apelike than human. Yet unlike apes, it can swim, see in the dark, and survive in a wide variety of climates. It makes eerie sounds, but has not developed a language, and it has great physical strength.

Green believes it does not prey on humans, but "a lone human attacked by a Sasquatch might not be able to return to tell the story."

Richard Beeson of the University of Idaho is sure there is no cause for worry. He has analyzed Sasquatch literature and studied human behavior. He thinks some of the people who report sightings are lying. The rest have been influenced by their own fears into thinking they saw something that doesn't exist.

Beeson concludes: "What the Sasquatch represents, I believe, is a modern form of myth and we are privileged to be able to see it in the making."

Does this mean that Bigfoot, this hairy creature

Researchers from the Bigfoot Center in Oregon head out on a trip to look for evidence for Bigfoot.

"A strong case can be made that our media have, in effect, created the Bigfoot phenomenon. Even a child can see how readily the subject lends itself to sensationalism."

Kenneth Wylie, anthropologist

"Everything on earth has not been discovered."

Odette Tchernine, author

that haunts lonely roads and leaves huge footprints, is nothing but a fairy tale?

"No!" says Dr. Myra Shackley. "In the light of the sheer wealth of reasonably reliable information that is now being gathered, there is a gradual change in scientists' attitudes, and something of a 'no smoke without fire' approach is emerging." As further evidence of a change in attitude, she says that, "Learned societies approve Bigfoot studies, and universities sponsor conferences.

"Indeed the Sasquatch is now respectable, and it is thought to be narrow-minded not to believe in its existence."

Still, until a Bigfoot—or its bones—is brought in for study, the mystery of the wilderness monsters will not be solved.

Will the elusive Bigfoot ever be found?

For Further Exploration

Norma Gaffron particularly recommends the following books for readers interested in learning more about Bigfoot.

Blumberg, Rhoda, *Monsters*. New York: Franklin Watts, 1983.

Bord, Janet and Colin, *The Bigfoot Casebook*. Harrisburg, PA: Stackpole Books, 1982.

Byrne, Peter, *The Search for Bigfoot*. Washington, DC: Acropolis Books, Ltd., 1975.

Cohen, Daniel, *America's Very Own Monsters*. New York: Dodd, Mead & Co., 1982.

Cohen, Daniel, *Monsters: Giants and Little Men from Mars*. Garden City, NY: Doubleday and Co., Inc., 1975.

Dolan, Edward F. Jr., *Great Mysteries of the Ice and Snow*. New York: Dodd, Mead & Co., 1985.

Hillary, Sir Edmund, and Doig, Desmond, *High in the Thin Cold Air*. Garden City, NY: Doubleday and Co., Inc., 1962.

Hunter, Don, with Dahinden, René, *Sasquatch*. New York: The New American Library, Inc., 1975.

Izzard, Ralph, *An Innocent on Everest*. New York: E.P. Dutton and Co., Inc., 1954.

Landsberg, Alan, *In Search of Myths and Monsters*. New York: Bantam, 1977.

Napier, John, *Bigfoot*. New York: E.P. Dutton and Co., Inc., 1973.

Patterson, Roger, *Do Abominable Snowmen of America Really Exist?* Yakima, WA: Franklin Press, 1966.

Place, Marian T., *On the Track of Bigfoot*. New York: Dodd, Mead & Co., 1974.

Rudley, Stephen, *The Abominable Snowcreature*. New York: Franklin Watts, 1978.

Sanderson, Ivan T., *Abominable Snowman: Legend Come to Life*. Philadelphia: Chilton Company, Book Division, 1961.

Tchernine, Odette, *The Snowman and Company*. London: Trinity Press, 1961.

Wise, William, *Monsters of North America*. New York: G.P. Putnam's Sons, 1978.

Wylie, Kenneth, *Bigfoot*. New York: The Viking Press, 1980.

Additional Bibliography

Antonopulos, Barbara, *The Abominable Snowman*. Milwaukee: Raintree Press, 1977.

Cohen, Daniel, *The Encyclopedia of Monsters*. New York: Dodd, Mead, & Co., 1982.

Coleman, Loren, and Clark, Jerome, *Creatures of the Outer Edge*. New York: Warner Books, 1978.

Dolan, Edward F. Jr., *The Bermuda Triangle and other Mysteries of Nature*. New York: Franklin Watts, 1980.

Guenette, Robert and Francis, *The Mysterious Monsters*. Los Angeles: Sun Classic Pictures, Inc., 1975.

Halpin, Marjorie, and Ames, Michael, *Manlike Monsters on Trial*. Vancouver and London: University of British Columbia Press, 1980.

Heuvelmans, Bernard, and Porshnev, Boris, *On the Track of Unknown Animals*. New York: Hill and Wang, 1965.

Hitching, Francis, *The Mysterious World*. New York: Holt, Rinehart, and Winston, 1978.

Izzard, Ralph, *The Abominable Snowman*. Garden City, New York: Doubleday and Co., 1955.

Krutch, Joseph, *The Most Wonderful Animals that Never Were*. Boston: Houghton Mifflin Co., 1969.

Matthiessen, Peter, *The Snow Leopard*. New York: The Viking Press, 1978.

Roosevelt, Theodore, *The Wilderness Hunter*. New York: G.P. Putnam's Sons, 1893.

Shackley, Myra, *Still Living? Yeti, Sasquatch and the Neanderthal Enigma*. New York: Thames and Hudson, Inc., 1983.

Slate, B. Ann, and Berry, Alan, *Bigfoot*. New York: Bantam, 1976.

Sprague, Roderick and Krantz, Grover S., *The Scientist Looks at the Sasquatch II*. Moscow, ID: University of Idaho Press, 1977.

Periodicals

Russ Kinne, ''The Search Goes on for Bigoot,'' *Smithsonian*, January 1974.

John Masters, ''The Abominable Snowman,'' *Harper's*, January 1959.

Minnesota Archaeologist, 1979. (Report of Bigfoot sightings and tracks in Iowa.

James B. Shuman, ''Is There an American Abominable Snowman?'' *Reader's Digest*, January 1969.

Index

Picture Credits

Photo/Patterson/Gimlin © 1968. Dahinden, 13, 73 all, 77 bottom, 99
Photos by René Dahinden. © Dahinden, 14 top, 15, 20 bottom, 23, 24, 30, 32, 70 both, 77 middle, 84
AP/Wide World Photos, 14 bottom, 28, 31, 61, 64, 74, 95
Peabody Museum, Harvard University. Photo by Hillel Burger, 16
Mary Ahrndt, 17, 44, 45, 55, 57, 63, 86, 87, 88
Bettmann Newsphotos, 18, 26, 27 right, 34, 38, 83, 90
John Green, 19, 69 left
Photos by Peter Byrne, Fellow, Royal Geographic Society, 20 top, 33, 69 right, 85, 89, 93, 97
© Librairie Plon 1955. Reprinted with permission of Georges Borchardt, Inc., Literary Agency, 35
Photos by John Beckett/London, 36 left & right, 37 left & right
Michigan/Canadian Bigfoot Information Center, 39, 40
Photo from *High in the Thin Cold Air* by Sir Edmund Hillary. © 1962 by Field Enterprises Educational Corporation. Reprinted by permission of Doubleday, a division of Bantam, Doubleday, Dell Publishing Group, Inc., 43
Courtesy British Information Service, 46
R. Satakopan/Sports Illustrated © Time, Inc., 47
Royal Geographic Society, 48, 50 left & right
Courtesy Minneapolis Public Library Picture Collection, 52, 53
From *The Abominable Snowmen: Legend Come to Life* by Ivan T. Sanderson, 56
Loren Coleman/Fortean Picture Library, 58, 78 right & left
Oscar & Associates, Inc., for World Book Encyclopedia, 62
Photo Researchers, Inc. © 1977 Bruce Roberts, 66
Tom McHugh/Photo Researchers, Inc., 67
TM & © 1977 Lucasfilm Ltd. All Rights Reserved. Courtesy of Lucasfilm, Ltd., 75 all, 76 all
© by Amazing Horizons/Sygma, 77 top
From *Bigfoot, the Yeti and Sasquatch in Myth and Reality* by John Napier, published 1973 by E.P. Dutton, 79
International Society of Cryptozoology, 81 all
Photo by Dr. Daniel W. Fry, supplied by the Amalgamated Flying Saucer Clubs of America, 91

About the Author

Norma Gaffron, a former school teacher, lives in New Brighton, Minnesota. She has been writing professionally for the past eleven years. Her articles, on topics as diverse as sailing, snakes, and replanting lost teeth, have appeared in many national magazines. She has been a Junior Great Books leader and is regional advisor for the National Society of Children's Book Writers.

Norma and her husband have three grown children. When the children were young, the family used to go camping in northern Minnesota, but not so far into the woods that they ever saw a Bigfoot or its tracks. Still, Norma loves mystery, challenge, and a bit of risk. She might even like to see a Bigfoot if given the chance.

Bigfoot: Opposing Viewpoints is Norma's second book in the Great Mysteries series. Her first was *The Bermuda Triangle*. She is currently researching unicorns and writing a novel about a girl who stows away on board a ship.